Peter Bromhead

Emeritus Professor of Politics, University of Bristol

Life in Modern Britain

6. 1. 89.

Longman

Longman Group UK Limited,
Longman House, Burnt Mill, Harlow,
Essex CM20 2JE, England
and Associated Companies throughout the world.

© Peter Bromhead 1962
© Longman Group Limited 1971, 1974, 1979, 1985
All rights reserved; no part of this publication may
be reproduced, stored in a retrieval system or transmitted
in any form or by any means, electronic,
mechanical, photocopying, recording or otherwise,
without the prior written permission of the Publishers.

First published 1962
Second edition 1964
Third edition 1971
Fourth edition 1974
Fifth edition 1979
Sixth edition 1985
Fourth impression 1987

Set in 12/13 pt Bembo 'Monophoto' Lasercomp.

Produced by Longman Group (FE) Ltd
Printed in Hong Kong

ISBN 0-582-74919-0

Acknowledgements

We are grateful to the following for permission to reproduce copyright material:

The author and New Society for an extract from an article 'School Rituals' by Ronald King from *New Society* 12/7/73, extracted by permission from New Society 12/3/73.

We are grateful to the following for permission to reproduce copyright illustrations:
Associated Press Ltd for page 205; Barnaby's Picture Library for pages 157, 168 (top); British Tourist Authority for page 198; Bertram W. Chapman for page 86 (top); Clifford Culpin and Partners (photo by Hank Snoek) for page 60; Cumbernauld Development Corporation for page 194 (bottom); Department of the Environment for page 52; Harlow Development Corporation for page 130 (top); John Hillelson for page 14; Home Office for page 79 (Crown Copyright – reproduced with permission of the Controller of Her Majesty's Stationery Office); Independent TV News Ltd for page 189; Joan Johnson for page 140; Keystone Press Agency Ltd for pages 33, 86 (bottom), 142 (bottom); Sheelah Latham/Ron Chapman for page 194 (top); Lawdon Ltd for page 118 (bottom); Eamonn McCabe for page 100; Popperfoto for page x (top), 168 (bottom), 210 (top and bottom); Press Association Ltd for pages 84, 165, 207 (top and bottom); Schweppes Ltd for page 190; The Scotsman for page 83; The Times for page x (bottom); Topix for page 158; Janine Wiedel for page 118 (top).

Cover photograph by Image Bank (Gerald Brimacombe)

We are unable to trace the copyright holders of the photographs on pages 60 (top), 86 (top), 100, 118 (top and bottom), 130 (top), and 194 (top). We would be grateful for any information that would enable us to do so.

To Alison and Marjory-anne

Preface

This book attempts to present a picture of the British country and people as they are at the present period, in the second half of the twentieth century. Its main objective is to convey information about the political, social and economic arrangements by which the British people manage their affairs. History is kept to a minimum. The emphasis is mainly on the features of British life which seem to be distinctive or characteristic of Britain rather than of Western Europe as a whole, or which seem likely to be of special interest to observers from outside. It is not my purpose to praise or to blame, to attack existing institutions or to defend them, to suggest reforms or to argue that reforms are not needed, but rather to present the facts as objectively as possible. Inevitably the process involves some choice of emphasis in which subjective elements must have some influence. The life of the British community, like that of any other, has its difficulties and its irrationalities, and many features which produce friction and dissatisfaction among elements of the British people themselves. Without some recognition of these the whole picture would be lifeless and inadequate, so wherever the facts suggest problems, I try to indicate what the problems are and to discuss them.

Great Britain is an island on the outer edge of the European continent, and its geographical situation has produced a certain insular spirit among its inhabitants, who tend, a little more perhaps than some other people, to regard their own community as the centre of the world. The insularity produces a certain particularism among the numerous groups of whom the whole community is composed. Every Briton, in so far as his life has various aspects corresponding with his work and his personal interests, is involved in several different particular groupings. But each group tends to produce its own special language to describe its own activities, a language which cannot be easily understood even by other Britons.

Some features of life are commonly described by special terms, and these terms, such as 'Justice of the Peace' and 'Public School', must be used and explained; but this book avoids the private jargon through which, for example, social scientists, social workers and many other groups tend to emphasise their professionalism.

Serious difficulties of definition remain. The British tend to avoid precise definition whenever they can. Only a few of the powers and functions of governmental institutions are defined by statute-law; most are based on unwritten conventions and accepted practices whose exact meaning is both uncertain and changing. Many other aspects of life are similarly obscure or subject to varying interpretations.

Within the 1970s there have been major structural reforms in the system of local government, the courts of law, the National Health Service, and the Civil Service. Since 1979 the state has reduced its participation in the economy, but the trade unions have asserted new powers. Real class–differences have been reduced, yet class antagonism has grown. Self-inflicted national economic failure, in comparison with the rest of Europe, has made further progress, and Britain's membership of the European Community has become more insular. So much has changed since 1978–9, when this book was last revised, that this new edition incorporates a great deal of new material, some of it factual and some to take into account new problems and new ideas.

This book owes a great deal to the help of many friends, mainly in Britain and in Sweden. To them I should like to express my gratitude for all their help. For new approaches in this sixth edition I should like particularly to express my debt to colleagues in the University of Graz and elsewhere in Austria, and to my wife and daughters.

Contents

Above: The Prince and Princess of Wales ride through London after
their wedding.
Below: A view of the Lake District.

1

The Country and the People

To others and themselves the British have a reputation for being conservative—not in the narrow political sense, but in the sense of adherence to accepted ideas, and unwillingness to question them. The reputation comes partly from their history. For 900 years they have suffered neither invasion nor revolution (except in 1649 and 1688) nor disastrous defeat in war. Their monarchy survives without serious question. Under its nominal leadership the political arrangements have been so stable that, except for two interruptions in the seventeenth century, they have been adapted through the centuries to meet changing needs without violent change. Britain in 1984 was unique in managing without a written constitution; some fragmentary definitions of 1688 still survived. There had been bitter quarrels, social and economic as well as political, but the quarrels had been settled, usually by compromise.

The underlying continuity had not been broken. The greatest empire ever seen had been built up, administered mainly with humanity and fairness. Then it was dismantled deliberately and without panic. Imperial power was ended with (on the whole) good will and dignity. At home the monarchy survived, almost universally admired, from habit rather than from specific rationalisation, though a rational defence of it could easily be found. Along with it there was still an hereditary aristocracy, still the object of some residual social deference, still entitled to speak and vote in an archaic House of Lords, yet by now denied almost all power in that House.

In the 1860s Walter Bagehot wrote about two special qualities of the British. He called them 'stupidity' and 'deference'. 'Stupidity' included a tendency to accept established values without questioning their validity. By 'deference' he meant the readiness of each social stratum, in a highly stratified society, to acknowledge the superiority of higher social strata, each in its predetermined place, though deference was complicated by the fluidity of the strata. The hereditary aristocracy may have scorned the newly-rich men of commerce, but it quickly absorbed them and their money through mutually useful marriages; and the old aristocrats moved into the new world of business as quickly as the newly-rich businessmen bought land and horses and sporting guns. Social stratification was not rigid, and deference was paid to achieved position once it was securely established.

In the twentieth century Bagehot's old deference has waned, along with the social and economic differences which sustained it. Economic inequality has been reduced, first steadily then rapidly. The war of 1939 had a revolutionary effect in reducing inequality, and this reduction was first found acceptable, then sustained for most aspects of life except housing, until the growth of unemployment in the 1980s. A typical senior surgeon may have had ten servants when Bagehot wrote; now he is likely to have none at all, and his home is equipped with the same kind of washing machine as that of the hospital porter with whom he exchanges polite 'good mornings'.

The surgeon's take-home pay may be three times the porter's now, instead of twenty times a hundred years ago, and the gulf between them has been reduced both by egalitarian values and by the numerous rights and concessions won by the porter's union; but nothing can change the difference in skill and responsibility between the porter's work and the surgeon's. The difference in status is likely to be reinforced by big differences of taste, reading, personal contacts and interests. The surgeon almost certainly owns his home, which is likely to be in a 'residential area' in town or suburb, or in a country village; wherever it is, other people of similar status have their homes nearby. The porter is more likely to live in what is known as a working class area, most probably as a tenant in a council estate, surrounded by others of status more or less similar to his own.

There is no doubt that perception of class differences is peculiarly significant in Britain. Political life is dominated by two parties, based more solidly on class than the equivalent two major parties in, for example, West Germany or the United States.

Perceptions of class differences are based partly on the past, partly on myths, partly on clearly-observable characteristics of present-day society. Ownership of property is an important factor, though in fact income from ownership of the means of production forms a very small proportion of the whole net incomes of even the richest one per cent of people aged below 65. Job-status, tastes and habits are much more significant components, along with personal contacts. Residential areas of British towns and suburbs are highly stratified, so that most neighbourhoods have a class flavour.

Significant class difference depends in fact above all on the distinction between manual and non-manual workers, usually called working class and middle class. About three-fifths of the population of working age are manual workers. Most manual workers support the Labour Party, most others support the Conservatives; but the proportion of manual workers who vote Conservative is in general bigger than that of the others who vote Labour. Between a quarter and a third of manual workers vote Conservative. Political scientists of the 1960s found evidence suggesting that working-class conservatism had its roots in the vestiges of Bagehot's deference: a trust in a party identified with an élite which, though much changed through adaptation, could trace its ancestry back to Bagehot's time. In 1983 the Labour Party emphasised class consciousness and resentment, and fewer than half of manual workers voted Labour.

The objects of deference and envy are not well defined. In 1959 one author wrote of 'The Establishment', using an old French analogy when he identified four hundred families still dominant through land ownership and the City of London—yet ready to admit newcomers to its group. This small élite, with a large hereditary element, dominated politics up to 1900 and still dominated the Conservative Party in the 1950s; not so now. It is still pre-eminent in banking and insurance; members of the cousinhood earn large directors' fees for doing work which still allows them to go to the horse races at Royal Ascot on working days in June. Some give some time to the House of Lords, a few are elected members of the House of Commons, many have leading positions, by election or appointment, in the counties where they have their country homes—and where they spend much time.

The notion of 'the rich' is broader. It includes the self-made men of the present generation; perhaps it includes the élite of the world of entertainment—managers as well as performers. But in a much wider sense the rich, as the objects of envy, are more diffuse. In the popular imagination they include those who have reached leading positions in industry—and ultimately all who achieve professional

success. At another level, resentment is directed at those with privileged education, or who use the English language in the manner associated with the privileged class.

Some hostile Marxist rhetoric is directed at the 'capitalists' who own that part of the means of production which is not yet owned directly by the public. 'The interests of capital and labour are fundamentally irreconcilable', said Hugh Scanlon, as chief of the engineering union, on television in 1977. In fact, by 1978 far more than half of the privately-owned capital of large companies was owned by contributors to institutions such as pension funds and life insurance policies; and these contributors were in fact the majority of the working population, both manual and white collar, including many members of Mr Scanlon's union. About one-third of the means of production was owned by some three million individuals, mainly aged over 65, some of them poor. Rich individual capitalists owned a scarcely significant proportion, and paid up to 98% tax on their dividends. But the surviving vestiges of traditional capitalism still provided the basis of a mythology which shaped attitudes to work and the whole social system.

The mythology is supported by the fact of hierarchy within large units of production. Not only surgeons in hospitals but holders of upper positions in all hierarchies, directors, higher executives, engineers and accountants, are easily identified with the mythical bourgeoisie even though they may themselves in fact be landless wage-earners, holding their positions through promotion by hard work, others by skill or effortless achievement, others by sycophancy, others by having been educated at the right school or by family connections, many by more than one of these. Within the business they have visible privileges, responsibility and power; they are an élite.

There is not now one single élite in Britain, there are many; in manufacturing and commerce, in press and entertainment, in law, accountancy and medicine, in local and central government administration. All these élites are graded, partly by age; and the multiplicity of élites is complicated by the existence of sub-groups, each with its own set of loyalties.

By 1984 individual ownership of shares in companies had continued to decline, while the business of investment managers of trusts, insurance companies and pension funds had grown. Meanwhile wage differentials had increased, to the advantage of the managers. Tax rates on the higher incomes had been drastically reduced. More than three million people were currently without work. Far more than these were in fear of unemployment, and many had experienced it. Although all classes were affected in some degree, the effects were most drastic among manual workers. Class inequalities had increased, in favour of people enjoying the greater security of middle-class jobs. Meanwhile, statistics were produced showing a long-term growth of inequality on one criterion. In thirty years, deaths before the age of 64 had increased substantially among unskilled manual workers, while among professional and managerial men they had declined; the gap between the two groups of men had doubled.

The British like to think that they excel in the qualities of moderation and tolerance. Such claims are obviously reinforced by the stability of government through several centuries, along with the maintenance of reasonable human rights and freedoms without a written constitution and without clear definitions. These qualities demand self-discipline and mutual respect among people. The miserable performance of the economy, the poor production record of British industry, the prevalence of strikes, the vandalism and the football hooligans of the 1980s—these and other negative features give ground for doubt whether the moderation and self-discipline are holding firm in modern times. But there are some grounds for optimism. Pedestrians cross streets against red lights when there are no cars coming, and nobody harasses them; but car-drivers obey the lights and regularly respect the pedestrian-crossings. Petty breaches of the law are tolerated when they are harmless and essentially justifiable. The death-rate on the roads is exceptionally low by European standards; statistically a car-traveller in France is three times as likely to be killed in a 100 kilometre trip as on the British roads.

With most other types of accidents, at work and in the home, the British record compares very favourably with almost all other European countries as well as the U.S.A. When Britain joined the European Community in 1972, rates of industrial accidents were as low as a third of those in Germany, a quarter of those in Italy. In the next ten years the British death rate from accidents at work was further reduced by half. These creditable figures appear to reflect a good capacity for self-discipline as well as effective enforcement of state-imposed regulations.

Accident statistics do not tell us everything about a people. But at least this little corner of the story, from the depressing 1980s, suggests that the old genius for Aristotelian moderation is not dead. The British may not be deferential any more, but they are usually polite, not according to rigid rules or practices of behaviour, but in conformity with the demands of mutual helpfulness. They suffer today from extremist politicians and trade union leaders—and distrust them. They also distrust both ideology and all rigid doctrines. If the British dislike both exactitude and all extremes, their attitude perhaps reflects the geography and climate of the island where they live. The British do not kill thrushes or blackbirds or sparrows. Cornish fishermen do not slaughter mackerel wholesale; nor are they happy when others deplete the sea to satisfy today's demands. In the past hundred years the British have done much to spoil their country, but they have done more to preserve its character, its green variety and its modest scale.

The United Kingdom includes four nations, and there are discernible differences between them. Both in Wales and in Scotland there are strong demands for more recognition of their national distinctness through the system of government. Each of these countries' people have always been more attached to the idea of social equality than the English, and in both there has been more equality of opportunity. Scotland has always fostered education on a democratic basis, and has always had a separate educational system. The Union with England preserved a separate legal system and distinct local administration; there are distinct Scottish customs and ways of speaking the English language. Wales has been assimilated administratively, but in recent years has been given special arrangements. But Welsh people (like the Scots) are more conscious of family connections than the English. Most Scottish and Welsh people live in small and heavily concentrated areas of coalmining and heavy industry (Glasgow – Edinburgh in Scotland, Glamorgan – Monmouthshire in South Wales), but they are very conscious of the mountains and empty spaces that cover most of their countries. Northern Ireland, similarly divided between industrial Belfast and a mountainous countryside, is tormented by differences between Protestants (who are strongly attached to England and Scotland) and the big Catholic minority whose sentimental links are with the Irish Republic.

Within England there are differences between the hard north, with its reputation for straight speaking and suspicion of hypocrisy, and the supposedly more artificial south. These differences are becoming less real than they were, with the increasing tendency of people to move from one part of the country to another. The higher one goes up the social scale, the less the regional differences. But the mere fact that the differences are supposed to exist keeps them alive to some extent.

The north is associated with the harsh heavy industries, coalmining, iron and steel and textiles, that developed in the nineteenth century, in Lancashire, Yorkshire, and the far north-east—and with the bare, cold, steep hills of the Pennines. Together these influenced the life of the people. The south of England has always been less definable. Some of it is flat, some undulating, but except for the moorlands of the south-west the hills are no more than 300 metres high. The countryside is green and tame, with small fields and high hedges. Outside London there are few large towns, but small towns and suburbs spread and wander everywhere, so that the countryside has a townish feeling.

This dynamic southern and south-eastern area is, not surprisingly, more prosperous than the rest of the country. Relatively fewer people leave school at sixteen, fewer die of bronchitis, more are in the two highest social classes. In spite of the great increase of population, fewer people live in overcrowded homes than in the midlands and north. (London itself is bad in some of these respects.) Although much new industry has been developed in the 'dynamic' south, only a third of the people are engaged in the manufacturing industry, as compared with half in the midlands and north.

Although England is so small a country the distances within it always seem to be greater than one would expect. This is partly because quite a short journey brings many changes of scene, partly because the crowding of so many people into so small an area makes travelling rather slow. England itself has 46 million inhabitants in 50,000 square miles (125,000 square kilometres) —nearly the same population as France, which is more than four times as big. Wales with 2,700,000 people in 8,000 square miles, and Scotland, with 5,000,000 in 30,000 square miles, are less crowded. Round London and Manchester and Birmingham, one can travel quite long distances without ever being clear of houses, but there are still some parts of the country which are empty and wild.

England is highly industrialised and was the country in which the earliest developments of modern industry took place. Many of the great inventions which were the foundation of modern industrial processes were made by Englishmen or Scotsmen, and there were men at the same time who possessed the vision and ability to put

7

the new inventions to use. The original basis of British industry was coalmining, and the early factories grew up not far from the main mining areas. Glasgow and Newcastle upon Tyne, each on a convenient river, became great centres of engineering and shipbuilding. Lancashire produced cotton goods and south-west Yorkshire woollens, with Sheffield concentrating on iron and steel. Birmingham and the other towns of the midlands developed light engineering, and later became the chief centre for making vehicles. More recently, oil has taken the place of coal for many purposes, and the oil under the North Sea should last for some years after 1990. The world does not go to Britain to buy textiles or ships as it did in the past. New light industry, much more diversified, has grown up in place of the old, and much of it cannot be so conveniently situated in the old industrial north. All regions are becoming less specialised, but the new industrial growth has been mainly in the south and midlands. The population in these areas is growing fast. Government action is encouraging new industries in the old areas, and without it the relative decline of the north would be faster still.

The central parts of the old industrial areas, with their long rows of red-brick houses, are still rather ugly and grimy. In 1975 the Government began seriously to promote 'urban renewal'. Because of the Clean Air Act of 1956 there is less pollution, and far less smoke, than in the past, but a hundred years of winter fogs have left their mark. In some ways it is unfortunate for England that so much of the earliest industrial development took place here. Those responsible for the growth of the factories in the nineteenth century had to make their own plans and could not learn from the mistakes of others. It was in and around Manchester in the middle of the century that Friedrich Engels found such impressive evidence of what he interpreted as the horrors of capitalism, while his collaborator Karl Marx worked over his books and papers in the British Museum in London.

By now the really bad slums of the central areas of towns have mostly been cleared, and the complaints of today are often directed against dullness and monotony. Nearly all English people now live in towns or suburbs and most towns are very like one another. Big cities have fine shops and streets of fairly high office-blocks, with the various architectural styles of the past hundred years mixed up together, but for the most part town streets are dominated by the shop-fronts of Littlewoods, Marks and Spencers, Boots and supermarkets which have branches in every town, each with its arrangement repeated in each place, and by a few cinemas and classical bank buildings. Round the centres are the factories, the new high blocks of flats and the surviving rows of nineteenth-century red-brick houses in their long, monotonous terraces, and further out still the newer estates of council houses, built by the public authorities, and the lines of semi-detached villas with their neat and well-kept gardens. Each year more of the country is occupied by these decent but dull developments and the town centres are dead at night.

Much of what is most pleasing in England has been left to us by pre-industrial society, or by the expenditure in the countryside of the profits made by the industry of the towns. England has a very rich architectural heritage. The greatest of the cathedrals and abbeys, built between 1100 and 1500, are in towns which have not become industrial centres and preserve their old character, so that the cathedrals themselves stand surrounded by expanses of grass and fine old private houses, in a setting not often equalled in continental Europe. From the same period there survive many fine parish churches, with their spires or towers rising peacefully above the surrounding trees. Outside the industrial areas the countryside is remarkable for the wonderful variety of shades of green in the fields and the trees—a delicacy and subtlety of colour not to be found in other places, and reflecting the lack of extremes in the climate. The streets of old market towns and country villages are often infinitely pleasing and harmonious, with the half-timbered houses of the sixteenth century in the south and midlands, the seventeenth-century stone of the Cotswold hills to the west of Oxford, and the dignified town terraces of the eighteenth and early nineteenth centuries in many parts of the country. Some of the best examples of this wonderful period of English architecture are to be seen in bigger towns like Bristol, Bath and Brighton.

Several hundred glorious country houses still survive from the eighteenth century and before. Most of the biggest of these, with their old furniture and paintings, have become in effect museums, and their glorious gardens are open to the public. Some are still owned by the families who have inherited them; typically they keep a few rooms for their private use and cover the cost of maintenance with the help of the admission fees paid by thousands of visitors each year. Many other houses have been bought and kept alive by the National Trust, a non-state organisation founded in

9

1895 to preserve the best of the nation's heritage.

The National Trust is financed partly by entrance fees paid by visitors to its houses, partly by gifts, legacies and the subscriptions of its 600,000 members. It owns and preserves not only houses and their gardens, but vast areas of moorland and mountain and 600 kilometres of coastline, all kept open to the public. Since 1945 the state has designated ten areas of wild coast or mountain as National Parks, and thirty-three smaller, less remote sections of country as Areas of Oustanding Natural Beauty, with severe restrictions on new quarries, industry or house-building; but little of this state activity would have been successful if it had not been based on a foundation established long before.

Britain has a great length of coastline, and no place is more than three hours from the sea by car—except during weekend traffic-jams. Britain's nineteenth century prosperity produced, in Brighton, Bournemouth and Blackpool, three of Europe's four biggest seaside-resort towns, along with a dozen others, each now with 50,000 to over 100,000 residents, many of them retired. In summer their beaches and amusements are crowded with day-visitors. Sixteen million people visited Blackpool in 1976. Some resorts were once thought to be 'fashionable'; such a notion would now seem absurd, even for Eastbourne or Torquay.

Away from the resort towns the best parts of the coast are now protected against any new building or development, and the glorious scenery of the cliffs and bays and coves of the south-west and South Wales has been made accessible by continuous public coastal footpaths. The paths are rough, and the few energetic people who walk along them can easily find solitude.

The Lake District, in the north-west, is commonly accounted the most beautiful part of England. Everything is on a small scale, and the hills look higher than they really are. It seems that before the beginning of the romantic movement in the late eighteenth century people were little concerned with scenic beauty, but that period produced Wordsworth and the other Lake poets, inspired by the perfection of water, trees and heather-covered slopes.

No discussion of English town and country would be complete without some special mention of London, the great centre of commerce, administration and culture which with its suburbs contains a fifth of all English people, and more than the whole of Scotland and Wales together. Like most capital cities London is taken by many foreigners to represent the whole country, and yet is untypical of the whole, with its variety and cosmopolitanism. London has changed a great deal in the past thirty years, and is now perhaps more tolerant and easy-going than it used to be, with its society less consciously stratified. Far fewer people live in its central areas than fifty years ago; the old East End had 600,000 people in 1921, but 200,000 now. The Clean Air Act of 1956 has put an end to the yellow-black winter fogs, and in thirty years the average winter sunshine has doubled.

A large proportion of the more prosperous city workers now have their houses in distant suburbs, but there are a few rather small fashionable residential districts in the 'West End'—though Mayfair, south of Oxford Street, now mostly consists of offices. Many districts, even near the centre, have a small-town life of their own, and some are dominated by people of a particular national origin—though not necessarily for more than a generation. The son of an East-European Jewish immigrant of fifty years ago, leaving his comfortable suburb to visit his East End childhood home, found the old Yiddish notices gone, replaced by signs in Bengali.

So much impermanence, change and movement have made the people more innovative, the place more lively, so full of surprises that nothing is surprising. The half million new inhabitants from the West Indies, Africa, India and Pakistan have contributed much to the new atmosphere. Many new trends have begun in London and spread through Europe, and their origin has been among the ordinary people. The umbrellas and bowler hats of the staid old London are still there, but they do not own the place any more.

From one generation to the next, London and Paris seem to have changed places. The editors of the Michelin guide still distribute their signs of excellence much more liberally to Paris restaurants, and there are still more French restaurants in London than English restaurants in Paris; but London is richer in variety because people from every corner of the world run its restaurants. In France's stagnant decades before the 1950s a Londoner could well compare the slow, smelly, dirty Paris Metro unfavourably with London's Underground; today the comparison is the other way round. Yet foreigners flock to London, drawn by its new and colourful reputation, in a way which astonishes its older inhabitants.

Only fifty years ago—and for centuries before—British people were the world's most active tourists, though not many foreigners visited Britain. In 1970 foreign visitors spent as much in Britain as British people spent abroad; by 1977 nearly twice as much. One cause was of course the devaluation of the British currency; but there must have been positive attractions as well as low prices. Relative economic decline had not made the country miserable. Britain has no brilliant cooking and no Alps, and the sea is rather cold; but there are good reasons for admiring the architecture and the scenery, and for enjoying the tolerance and friendliness of the people.

The movement from the cities			
	population in thousands		
	1931	1961	1983
Liverpool	855	750	510
Manchester	770	660	450
Inner London	4400	3200	2350
Outer London	3800	5000	4400
Rest of South-East England	6200	9100	12100
Inner London as % of South-East as a whole	30	18	12

Question

Movement of this kind started later in some British cities, and is now affecting most large cities in France, Germany and the U.S.A. Why is it happening, and why did it start so early in parts of England?

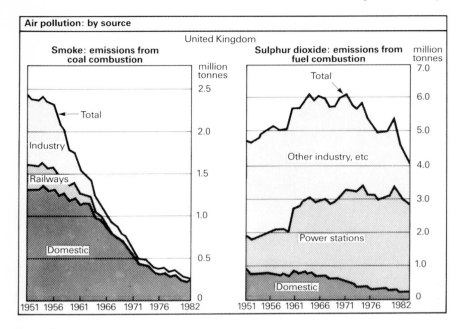

Air pollution: by source

United Kingdom

Smoke: emissions from coal combustion

Sulphur dioxide: emissions from fuel combustion

Question

Discuss the implications of these tables.

The Prime Minister, Mrs Margaret Thatcher.

2

Government and Politics

1 The Queen and the Constitution

For more than two hundred years the British system of government was admired for its combination of stability with adaptability, along with its avoidance of arbitrary power. In 1950 Britain was the most prosperous of the major European nations and apparently the most stable, with the most successful balance of authority and toleration.

By 1975 the old admiration had been weakened. British policies had not been stable or consistent. Their democratic basis had become dubious. In terms of material prosperity, in comparison with the rest of Europe, Britain had suffered an astonishing relative decline, self-inflicted yet not intended. All this had happened under that same political system which in the past had worked so well.

This chapter will describe the system and ask what has gone wrong. To do this, partly because there is no written Constitution, we must begin by looking at its origins in the 'glorious revolution' of 1688-9. This revolution put an end to arbitrary royal power, not by setting limits as in the later Constitutions of the American States, but giving the elected Parliament power to determine and control all the actions of the executive government. Absolute Sovereignty was not destroyed; it was placed firmly in the hands of 'The King-in-Parliament', with the idea that the duality would safeguard the people's freedom.

monarchy

The constitutional system, like the common law, is the result of a long process of growth. Each new problem has had to be solved somehow, and a solution once used tends to be used again unless those who decide see a good reason for acting differently. There is great respect for precedents, in Parliament, the administration and the courts of law.

Part of the constitutional system is based on precedent and

custom. 'Conventions' are unwritten rules or assumptions that have come to be accepted, though they have no defined authority. Some particular problems have been solved by legislation. Acts of Parliament (also called 'laws' or 'statutes') have defined a few aspects of the constitutional system, in particular the franchise and many other matters concerning elections—some of them in close detail. The Parliament Acts of 1911 and 1949 give the House of Lords only a small power to delay bills passed by the Commons; other Acts of 1876 and 1958 allow non-hereditary peers to be created, thus replacing an old custom by which all peerages were hereditary. These statutes have no special status. Like all the other forty to seventy Acts of Parliament passed each year they can be amended or repealed by new Acts of Parliament, which need no more in practice than a simple majority of those voting in the House of Commons (subject to a small delaying power of the House of Lords, hardly ever used).

Until the 1970s there was a general confidence in this vague system. There was no constitutional definition or guarantee of personal rights, no limit on the powers of the Queen-in-Parliament except those set informally by custom; the few fragmentary statutes could all easily be superseded. By the 1970s there were new grounds for fearing that the lack of definition might be dangerous. There were new demands for more effective protection against possible future threats; but nothing had been achieved by 1984.

In 1689 it was established that the hereditary monarch should be a Protestant, and that he or she should make laws, impose taxes and spend public money only with the consent of Parliament. The king appointed ministers to take charge of the departments of the Government; but as their policies needed money, and occasionally legislation, the logic of their position demanded that they should hold office only so long as the elected Parliament's majority accepted them. Already the House of Commons had insisted that it alone, and not the Lords, controlled finance.

The three main foundations of modern British government were built on the basis of the 1689 settlement in the eighteenth and nineteenth centuries, without deliberate plan. First, each minister was 'responsible' to the House of Commons, which could force him to resign. Second, the responsibility of the ministers was 'collective'; unless one minister was disowned by his colleagues all shared jointly in the responsibility for each act of government. Third, the ministers all belonged to that party which held a majority of seats in the House of Commons; the minority party formed the Opposition and hoped, after the next general election, itself to form the Government because of a change in majority.

This basic system still survives. The Queen is part of it, but only in a formal sense. As it is often said: she reigns but does not rule. The State as a legal entity is commonly called 'the Crown'. The Queen is its embodiment; all ministers and officers of the central government are her servants. For legal purposes there are no British 'citizens', but only 'subjects'. As a constitutional monarch the Queen appoints the Prime Minister; normally the leader of the party with a majority in the Commons; but it seems to be accepted that the politicians should arrange things so that she does not have to make a real choice herself. In 1979, when Callaghan resigned because his Party (Labour) had lost the general election, the Queen automatically appointed Mrs Thatcher, who was the Leader of the Conservative Party, which had won an overall majority of the seats. Now that both major parties (and the Liberals) have formal procedures for electing their leaders (p.30), the Queen should never even seem to make a choice herself, unless there should be no party with an overall majority. This happened in 1974, and she appointed Wilson as the already-elected leader of the biggest party.

Having appointed a Prime Minister the Queen appoints other ministers and public servants on his★ advice, and gives the Royal Assent to bills passed by Parliament. It is a convention of the constitution that the Queen always acts only as her ministers tell her to. It is not clear what she should do if she received advice which seemed to her to be unconstitutional; the matter has not yet been put to the test. The absence of a written constitution would make it difficult to claim that any advice was 'unconstitutional'; and if the Queen should go against her ministers they could claim that her action was itself 'unconstitutional'.

Questions of this kind are hypothetical but interesting. It seems right to assume that in an extreme case the Queen might feel it to be her duty to insist on a new general election before agreeing to act in a way which seemed to her to be wrong. If the second house of Parliament is abolished in the 1980s (a plan approved in 1977 by the Labour Party Conference), the Queen will be the only remaining protection for the people against the possible excesses of a party holding power.

★Here and throughout, please assume 'his/her', 'he/she', etc.

Events of the 1970s gave cause for some uncertainty as to whether the system would work as successfully in the future as it had done in the past.

2   The Government

Effective power belongs to the Government, which is part of Parliament and responsible to it, but which also normally dominates it. The Government consists of about a hundred politicians under the Prime Minister, appointed to their offices, as ministers, whips, etc. by the Queen on his advice.

A modern Government is arranged in about fifteen departments, each with its ministerial head, normally entitled, for example, 'Secretary of State for Social Services'. The number changes from time to time, as departments are split or joined together. All the heads of departments are members of the House of Commons. Nearly every head of department has under him one, two or three 'ministers of state', and at a lower level one, two or three 'parliamentary under-secretaries'. Some of the offices have special titles, but the world 'minister' is commonly used to describe all these office-holders.

The Cabinet consists of the sixteen to twenty-four senior ministers whom the Prime Minister has appointed as members of it. These are the heads of the departments together with a few others. The Cabinet meets about once a week in Number 10 Downing Street, a rather ordinary house which also contains the Prime Minister's personal office. He lives on the top floor. Number 10 is not really as small as it looks; there are big extensions behind the house, and the whole group of buildings is used by the Cabinet Secretariat as well as the Prime Minister's own civil service group and political officers. Most ministers in the Cabinet are heads of departments. During the years 1960–80 the arrangement of the departments was changed many times. A new Department of the Environment absorbed local government, housing (and for a few years Transport). Social Services absorbed insurance and health. These amalgamations and others made it possible for all heads of departments to be included in the Cabinet.

Although the word 'minister' is used as a generic term, nearly all the ministers who are heads of departments now have the title 'Secretary of State'. There were fifteen of them in 1978, and the only department with a 'minister' as its chief was Agriculture. The minister in charge of finance still has the archaic title 'Chancellor of the Exchequer', and the Lord Chancellor is in charge of Justice. Several other archaic offices survive, but are now used for new purposes. The Lord President of the Council has in recent years been Leader of the House of Commons, the Lord Privy Seal, Leader of the House of Lords; these two are in charge of the management of business in their respective Houses.

A politician's career normally begins by election to the House of Commons where he remains for some years as a 'back-bencher'. If he is successful in convincing the party leader of his ability to hold ministerial office he will at last receive his first appointment as a junior minister in one of the offices of the lowest rank; then eventually he may be promoted up the ladder.

There are also other positions on the fringe of the Government, held by M.P.s or peers. Two M.P.s of the party in power are appointed Law Officers for England, two for Scotland; then there are Whips in both Houses, concerned with managing the business. It may be convenient to show these political offices in a table, as they were in 1984.

	M.P.s	Lords	Total
Members of the Cabinet	18	3	21
Other ministers/Ministers of State	19	7	26
Law officers	3	—	3
Junior ministers (Parliamentary Under-Secretaries)	26	4	30
Whips	14	7	21
Total	80	21	101

Thus we see that, out of the (usually) 320 to 350 M.P.s of the party in power, 80 hold some actual office. All these share in the whole Government's responsibility.

No minister of any rank is allowed to indicate disagreement with any aspect of settled Government policy, either in Parliament or on any public platform outside. If even a junior minister should criticise Government policy even in reply to a question from a member of the public during a political meeting in a schoolroom far from London on a Friday evening, the local press will report his indiscretion, the Opposition will hear of it, and in the next week the Prime Minister will have to answer an embarrasing question in the House of Commons. If any minister disagrees with any aspect of his Government's settled policy he must hide his disagreement and give loyal support. A policy which has been settled without a minister's knowledge, at a meeting where he was not present, is binding on him because he shares the whole Government's responsibility for all policy. If he will not accept his share of that responsibility he must resign.

The requirement of ministerial solidarity does not extend to matters about which the Government as such does not have a settled policy, or where the Government's policy is to leave the decision to a free vote of the House of Commons, with each individual M.P. voting according to his own preference. Until recently such exceptions were rare, except in matters commonly seen to involve personal conscience or religious sentiment. In the 1970s the exceptions have been extended to include some important issues of national policy, particularly those connected with Britain's part in the European Economic Community (E.E.C.).

A minister who resigns through disagreement with his Government's policy may give his reasons, and thereafter criticise his colleagues from the parliamentary back benches. Resignation often ends a politician's career as a leading politician, but not in every case. Eden, Macmillan and Wilson all resigned office and later came back with reputations strengthened; but each resigned for reasons in accord with party purity and in protest against compromise. It is probably more dangerous to resign on behalf of moderation than against it.

British government has traditionally been called 'Cabinet government', because of the collectivity of its members. The term dates from the nineteenth century, before the huge increase in the number of political ministers and under-secretaries of the lower levels. The oldest departments, notably Foreign and Defence, have their main offices in Whitehall, which is the name of the street which runs from Trafalgar Square to the Palace of Westminster, where the two Houses of Parliament have their home. The practice of describing the British Government as 'Whitehall' comes from the location of these old departments in this street—though with the huge growth of government in recent times other departments have their offices scattered about in the same area of London. But the increase of government has tended to enhance the Prime Minister's personal power in relation to other ministers. He is not 'Whitehall'; but he dominates Whitehall.

A secretary of state in charge of a modern department may have one or two political ministers of state and two or three junior ministers to help him, as well as more civil servants than the whole Government had 150 years ago. But the secretary of state has so much to do in his own department (not forgetting his work as M.P. for his constituency) that he cannot easily find time to think deeply about government policy as a whole. Because of this—and for other reasons too—the Prime Minister is well placed to dominate his government when he wishes to. He is in modern times built up by television, which tends to personalise politics; he is the effective equal of heads of foreign governments who are constitutionally more than first among equals; he has become party leader by defeating his most important rivals in a contest decided by the votes of his parliamentary party colleagues. He decides when the Cabinet will meet and what it will discuss—and what can be dealt with without reference to it.

No minister may refer outside to discussions that have taken place in the Cabinet or any of its committees. This rule follows from the principle of collective responsibility, involving all ministers equally. Ministers' memoirs and autobiographies must be inspected by officials who ensure that the rule is not breached. When the former Labour minister, Patrick Gordon-Walker, wrote an academic book, *The Cabinet*, he made changes in the text to satisfy the rules. Since then, however, the rules have been weakened. Wilson's book, *The Labour Government 1964–70*, gives more information about problems with his ministers than earlier memoirs; and so do the books written by his political secretary, Marcia Williams, and press secretary, Joe Haines. But the most extreme breach of secrecy of modern times is in the three-volume published diaries of Richard Crossman, who was in the Cabinet until 1970. The material in these books does not add to the reputation of British Cabinet government.

3   The Civil Service

When we speak of 'the Government' we tend to think of the ministers, who are politicians. But we must not forget that each department has a large staff of professional civil servants who do most of the work of running the department on the minister's behalf.

The Civil Service is wholly non-political. Those of its members who are in any way concerned with administration are forbidden to be candidates for Parliament or to give public support to any political party, though they may vote at elections. When a new government comes into office the same civil servants must work for the new ministers, who a few weeks before led the attack on the old ministers' policies.

Until 1970 the highest positions were held by members of the administrative class—people who entered the service after passing a highly competitive examination, of university degree standard, and then went up the ladder, some of them quickly, some slowly, chosen for promotion because of their good work. Most of the permanent secretaries and deputy secretaries in the departments were graduates of Oxford or Cambridge, and a high proportion had studied classics or history. Below the administrative class were the executive and the clerical classes, non-graduates most of whom entered the service after leaving school. Some people who began in these classes were promoted into the administrative class but few reached the highest posts. Specialists, such as lawyers, scientists or engineers, could give the administrators expert advice, but could not themselves become administrators.

For several years the old administrative class was criticised for being an èlite which was essentially amateur, advising ministers who were more amateur still about matters which required special knowledge. In 1968 a committee under Lord Fulton (a former Oxford tutor) was set up to examine the system, and the changes which it proposed have now been introduced. In 1970–72 the old classes were abolished, so that now every civil servant is eligible for promotion to any position—though those who enter as graduates (still by examination) are likely to go higher than the others. A civil service college was established, reflecting admiration for the French Ecole Nationale d'Administration. But its form is very different; young civil servants are trained for short periods, with an emphasis on economic studies, while others attend short courses during their careers.

By the 1980s it seemed that the 'Fulton reforms' had not had much effect. The top civil servants were still the same kind of people, working in the same way, as before the reforms of 1970. Some new devices had been tried. Within most departments ministers appointed their own political advisers to work alongside their top officials. In the 1970s Mr Heath had created a new group, the Central Policy Review Staff, to undertake special inquiries to help the Cabinet in forming its policies; but in 1982 Mrs Thatcher replaced this with a new Policy Unit more closely under her own direction.

Once a civil servant has an established post he has almost complete security of tenure, and can in practice only be removed for improper conduct. Promotion is not automatic according to seniority, but selective, and based on the recommendation of superior officers. A civil servant does not necessarily remain in the same department all through his career; in fact when a department has a vacancy in one of its top posts it is very likely that it will be filled by someone brought in from another department. The chief official of a department is the permanent secretary, and below him are under-secretaries, assistant secretaries and principals. The permanent secretary is in close touch with the minister, and has the task of issuing directives which will put the ministers' policies into force. Each civil servant must know exactly how far his personal responsibility extends, and what questions he ought to refer to someone higher up.

Many people say that Britain is really managed by the Civil Service, and that the ministers, being mere amateurs, just do what the civil servants tell them to do—or find themselves frustrated whenever they try to implement any new ideas. One of the main professional duties of the civil servant is to shield his minister from criticism in the House of Commons. Any innovation is likely to upset some established interest, which can be relied upon to feed some M.P. with material to attack it.

Genuine loyalty to the minister in office is the first element in the professionalism of any civil servant, skill in defending departmental positions is the second; and an ability to seem to reconcile the two, even when they conflict, demands intelligence, hard work and flexibility. A successful civil servant gets his reward: high pay, state honours and a right to an inflation-proof pension at sixty.

Is there, then, a danger that the privileged civil servants may be prejudiced against the Labour Party's claimed defence and championship of the underprivileged? Many Labour ministers have paid tribute to the support which they received from their officials, though recently a few have dissented. Labour ministers in office in 1964–70 and 1974–9 appointed increasing numbers of their own party political advisers to supplement their civil servants, and Conservative ministers, in their turn, have done the same, but on a smaller scale.

4 Elections

The foundations of the electoral system were laid in the Middle
Ages. Since then numerous Acts of Parliament have modified the
system but never in a systematic way. Fundamentally the system
still has its ancient form, with each community electing its (now)
one representative to serve as its Member of Parliament until the
next general election. If an M.P. dies or resigns his seat a by-
election is held to replace him. Any British subject can be
nominated as a candidate for any seat on payment of a deposit,
though peers, clergymen, lunatics and felons in prison are
disqualified from sitting in the House of Commons. There is no
need to live in the area or to have any personal connection with it,
and less than half of the candidates are in fact local residents. There
are usually more than two candidates for each seat, but the one who
receives most votes is elected. A large proportion are elected with
less than half of the votes cast.

The franchise (right to vote) became universal for men by stages
in the nineteenth century; hence the rise of the Labour Party.
Women's suffrage came in two stages (1918 and 1928), and in 1970
the minimum voting age was reduced to eighteen. Since 1948 each
voter has had only one vote, which he may cast at his place of
registration; if he knows that he will be unable to vote, because he
is ill or has moved away or must be away on business, he may
apply in advance to be allowed to send his vote by post.

Two changes were introduced in 1984. Until then any candidate
who received more than $12\frac{1}{2}$ per cent of the votes had his deposit of
£150 returned to him; otherwise he lost his deposit. When the
figure of £150 was first used it was more than a man's average
wage for a year: enough to deter irresponsible candidatures. By
1984, because of inflation, it was about a week's wage. Huge
numbers of individual candidates had stood for election, happy to
sacrifice their deposits as a small price for some publicity. For the
Finchley constituency in London at the general election of 1983 the
results were as follows:

	Votes	Per cent
Thatcher, Mrs M. (Conservative)	19,616	51.1
Spigel, L. G. (Labour)	10,302	26.8
Joachim, Dr Margaret (Liberal/Alliance)	7,763	20.2
Wilkinson, Ms S. (Women for Life on Earth)	279	0.7

Sutch, D. (Screaming Lord Sutch) (Loony Soc)	235	0.6
Noonan, A. J. (Ban Every Licensing Law Soc)	75	0.2
Anscomb, Miss H. (Independent)	42	0.1
Whitehead, A. P. (Law and Order)	37	0.1
Webb, D. A. (Anti-cen)	28	0.1
Wareham (Party of Associates with Licensees)	27	0.1
Wedmore, B. (Belgrano)	13	0.0

Under the new arrangement the deposit was increased to £1,000, but any candidate with more than five per cent of the votes would get his money back. Another small reform made it possible for a person to vote by post if he had already arranged to be away on holiday before the announcement of the date of the general election.

Voting is not compulsory, but in the autumn of each year every householder is obliged by law to enter on the register of electors the name of every resident who is entitled to vote. Much work is done to ensure that the register is complete and accurate, and each register is valid for one year beginning towards the end of February. People who are just too young to vote are included in the list, so that they may vote at any election which may be held after their eighteenth birthday. It is only possible to vote at the polling station appropriate to one's address.

In 1973–83 there were 635 M.P.s for the U.K., each representing one 'constituency'; in 1983 the number was increased to 650. Because some areas increase in population while others decline, the electoral map, or division of the whole country into constituencies, has to be changed from time to time so as to prevent gross inequalities of representation. The maximum interval between 'redistributions' is set by law at 15 years—each time subject to Parliament's approval.

When a new electoral map is needed, a new draft plan is prepared by impartial Boundary Commissioners for England, Wales, Scotland and Northern Ireland. They ensure that within each of these four areas each constituency has an electorate (i.e. population registered for voting) as near as practicable to the average. Constituency boundaries are not allowed to cut across the boundaries of counties (or, in London, boroughs). Variations up to

20 per cent above or below the average are acceptable and quite numerous. When a new map is drawn, the variations occur by chance and (except for some over-representation in Scotland, particularly its sparsely populated parts) do not consistently affect any particular type of area.

More important are the effects of population movement during the life of a map. Sine the 1950s the populations of London, Manchester and other big cities have almost all declined (Liverpool from 800,000 to 500,000 in thirty years), while most of the southern counties, outside their big towns, have doubled. So, during the life of an electoral map, the urban areas which lose people but keep the same constituencies become over-represented, at the expense of the growing areas outside cities, particularly in the South. Furthermore, a new draft map is subject to criticism, public examination and amendments, a process spread over several years. The map based on 1965 populations was not brought into effect until 1971, and not used for an election until 1974. Even then its constituencies were already nine years out of date. This 1965 map was used for the election of 1979 and was still effective in 1982, although a new draft map, based on 1976 populations, was under discussion. By 1982 the average electorate per constituency in the non-city parts of southern England was 86,000, as compared with around 50,000 for London, Manchester, Salford, Liverpool, Newcastle and Edinburgh, and 41,000 for Glasgow. In the under-represented non-city South, 15 M.P.s represented over 100,000 electors each; in the most central parts of the cities, 20 M.P.s had less than 40,000 electors each. The most important effect of the electoral system, with each seat won by the candidate with most votes, has been to sustain the dominance of two main rival parties, and only two. One forms the Government, the other the Opposition, hoping to change places after the next general election. The Prime Minister enjoys one special advantage: he can choose the date of an election, with only three or four weeks' notice, at any time that seems favourable to his party, up to five years after the last. At an election the people choose 'A Parliament' for five years and no more; but only one 'Parliament', so defined, has lasted its full five years since 1945. The shortest, elected in February 1974, was dissolved seven months later. The development of opinion polls gives the Prime Minister a good idea of his party's chances, month by month.

Until 1918 the Conservatives (Tories) and Liberals (formerly Whigs) took turns at holding power, then Conservatives and

Labour. The Labour Party, formed in 1900 in alliance with the Liberals, replaced them as the second major party after 1918.✗ Labour's success was made possible by divisions among the Liberals.

In 1945–83 there were twelve general elections. No party ever received as many as half of the votes cast, but eleven of the twelve elections gave an overall majority of seats to Labour (5) or Conservative (6); the winning party's percentage of the votes varied from 39% to 49%. The exception was in February 1974 when the biggest party in the House of Commons, Labour, had only 301 seats out of 635. A minority Labour Government took power. After only seven months Prime Minister Wilson called a second election, in the hope of obtaining an overall majority. With Labour winning 319 seats he just succeeded, though Labour had less than two fifths of the votes. Within two years Labour had lost five seats at by-elections, but stayed in office as a minority government through an agreement with the Liberals. This was not a coalition, but the only period since 1931 in which a governing party relied on the support of another to remain in power.

At the election of 1979 the Conservatives won 339 seats out of 635. The two-party system seemed fully restored, with the Conservatives comfortably in power; but the leftward drift of Labour in opposition led an important group of Labour M.P.s to defect and form a new party. The group, calling itself Social Democrat, soon made an agreement with the Liberals: at the next election each constituency would have either a Liberal or a Social Democrat candidate, and the two parties would form an alliance.

For part of 1981 the new alliance seemed to have broken the two-party system. According to several opinion polls, a general election at that time would have given the alliance almost twice as many votes as either Conservatives or Labour, and an overall majority in the House of Commons. But there was no election then. The Conservatives continued in power with the majority they had gained in 1979. After the Falklands war in 1982 they again took the lead in the opinion polls, and in June 1983 their Prime Minister, Mrs Thatcher, decided to hold an election before the new popularity ebbed away.

In terms of seats in Parliament the 1983 election fully maintained the two-party balance. Mrs Thatcher's Conservatives won 393 seats out of 650 and stayed in unchallengeable power. Labour with 209 seats formed the Opposition. The new Liberal-Social Democrat Alliance had only 23: little more than the total of Scottish

Nationalists (4) and Northern Irish (17, of which 11 for the main
Protestant party and 6 for four other Catholic or Protestant
minorities).

But in terms of votes cast by the people the two-party system
looked much less secure. The Conservatives' huge majority in seats
was obtained with only 42.4 per cent of the votes. The Alliance,
with 25.4 per cent, narrowly failed to beat Labour's 27.6 per cent.
In England Labour and Alliance were even more nearly equal, with
26.8 per cent and 26.4 per cent respectively—but 148 and 13 seats.
The results for the south of England were even more remarkable:

	per cent of votes	seats	per cent of seats
Conservative	51.3	224	86
Labour	19.98	29	11
Alliance	28.85	7	2.7

In the country as a whole, Alliance candidates came second in
309 constituencies, Labour only in 132, Conservatives in 170. The
wide spread of the support for this 'third' party ensured that the
electoral system worked to its extreme disadvantage. Before the
election it was calculated that if Labour, Conservative and Alliance
were equal in terms of votes, Labour would win 296 seats to the
Alliance's 69.

In Parliament and the affairs of the state, the two-party system
continued after 1983 as confidently as before. Labour, as the
Opposition, began the task of preparing for the next election,
probably in 1987 or 1988, with some hope of winning it. They
shared one purpose with the Conservatives: to keep unchanged the
electoral system which had served them both so well.

Many opinion polls, over many years, have indicated that most
of the British people would prefer to use their most fundamental
right, that of voting, in a system which would give fair
representation. But both Conservatives and Labour, whenever
either gains power, avoid electoral reform. Both claim that the
existing system is objectively better than any other, and produce
objective arguments for it and the two-party dominance which it
sustains. First, all the people of each constituency have one M.P. to
represent them and their interests. Second, the system gives the
people a clear choice between two alternative sets of leaders and

policies. Third, it gives stable government for up to five years at a time. Fourth, because any person with realistic political ambitions must join one of the two main parties, each party includes a wide range of attitudes. Therefore, fifth, each party's programme, being a compromise, is likely to avoid extremes—and a government knows that within five years of taking power it must again face the judgement of the voters.

On the other side it is pointed out that two-party choice at an election may be no better than a choice between two evils. Ministers of both parties, once in office, have developed a habit of claiming that at the last election the people voted to approve of every item in the winning party's election manifesto—although the truth is that only about two-fifths voted for the party, and many of these were more against the losers than for the winners. The claims about moderation, once well founded, have become less convincing in the past ten years or so—and both parties have lost the leading moderates from their front benches.

Under this electoral system, in the past fifty years, between three and five per cent of the House of Commons seats have been won by women. In Benelux, Germany, Italy, Denmark and Switzerland (since women were enfranchised there in 1971) the proportion has regularly been two to three times greater. Yet in a very detailed cross-national survey, women's participation in public affairs generally was found to be higher in Britain than in most of these countries. Unlike Britain, they all use proportional representation based on party lists. In West Germany more women are elected from the lists than in the single seats; in France the list system in 1946–58 produced more women deputies than the Fifth Republic's single seats. In the United States female participation in affairs generally is exceptionally high, but a single seat majority electoral system, like the British one, generally produces around three per cent of women in the U.S. House of Representatives, and fewer than this in the U.S. Senate.

In Britain, when a party's selectors are choosing a single candidate, they tend to exclude people of minority groups or with characteristics different from the usual; and this tendency is strongest in seats which a party expects to win. Yet women candidates do not get fewer votes than men in similar situations; their results, where they have been chosen, conform to the party voting patterns. The electors vote for a party, not caring much about the individual candidate.

5 The Conservative and Labour Parties

The Conservatives have always been the party of the Right, identified with the existing social order. The party's M.P.s alone elect their leader. Conservative values accept leadership in principle, and the party's leader, once in office, is accepted as the director of its policies. As Prime Minister he chooses and dismisses ministers, moves them from one department to another, with some consideration for the need to include among them representatives of the main strands of opinion in the party, and expects their loyal support. When in Opposition he does the same with his Shadow Cabinet.

The party's Central Office is responsible to the leader. The M.P.'s are expected to observe discipline and to vote with the Party at whipped votes on several nights a week, usually at 10 p.m., and it is assumed that hope of promotion to ministerial office provides them with an incentive for obedience. There is scope for an M.P. to try to influence his leader's policies by presenting arguments to Whips (and through them to ministers) and by speaking and seeking support at party M.P.s' specialist groups and at the M.P.s' weekly general meeting.

Outside Parliament the party has more than a million individual members who pay annual subscriptions, with an association for each constituency (reconstructed when constituency boundaries are changed). The most important function of an association is to choose the party's candidate for the next election, and then to keep in close touch with him as an M.P. if he is elected. The chief officers of the association have most influence; if the M.P. abstains or votes the wrong way in Parliament he may be asked to explain his action to a general meeting of the association or of its executive committe, and the ultimate sanction is a decision not to re-adopt him as candidate at the next election.

When a constituency needs a new candidate, there are usually several dozens of applicants, some local people, some from other areas, most of them already on the national list of approved candidates. Two or three officers of the association may choose up to twenty of the aspirants for interview, as though they were applicants for an ordinary job. Eventually, they reduce the list to about three or four for interview at a full meeting of the association's executive committee, which has usually between 50 and 100 or more members. The committee hears the aspirants speak and answer questions, one by one, then votes by exhaustive ballot until one is the winner. Male aspirants' wives come in with them because the Conservatives' world is full of social events. It can adapt itself to a woman M.P. (or mayor, prime minister or monarch) but a man alone is incomplete.

The National Union of Conservative Associations is the partner, in London, of the Central Office, on which it may exert pressure. Each autumn a few representatives of each local association go, with the M.P.s and national leaders, to a four-day conference at a seaside town. There, with continuous television coverage, each section of the nation's business is debated for an hour or two, on the basis of a motion formed from several local proposals, and voted on, usually by a show of hands with a conclusion supportive of the national leadership.

Those who go to the conference are the most dedicated Tories, and some opinions voiced there have been critical of the leaders for their readiness to compromise. In Mrs Thatcher the M.P.s chose the kind of leader favoured by the activists, and her radical policies have in general been well supported. Tory purists welcome the privatisation of sections of the nationalised industries, the sale of council houses, the rhetoric of the state's withdrawal from direction of the economy. They also favour a strong stance on the pursuit of the national interest, and a high priority for defence and law and order. They would be critical of an M.P. showing weakness on these matters (they call it 'wetness'). But many of these activists are also local councillors, and unhappy about the government's current interference with such autonomy as the councils have traditionally enjoyed.

The Labour Party's internal structure is in most ways like the Conservatives', but big differences arise from Labour's attempts to give much more real power to ordinary members. Labour's annual conference is the supreme policy-making body of the party, and the parliamentary leaders are expected to follow its general policies when in power or in opposition. During each annual conference the sections of the party choose, by vote, their 28 representatives on the National Executive Committee (N.E.C.) which makes decisions week by week. The N.E.C. includes the leader and, usually, several ministers (when in power) or shadow ministers who, in opposition, are elected by the M.P.s. Relations between the N.E.C. and Labour cabinets in office have often produced bitter arguments, much publicised in the newspapers.

The annual conference is attended by delegates from the constituency parties, trade unions and other bodies affiliated to the Labour Party. Each delegation's voting weight depends on the number of party members represented. In most trade unions most of the union members are automatically affiliated to the Labour Party. The union hands over some of the union subscriptions to the party. Any union member may 'contract out' of party membership, but many do not know of this; in 1984 the Trades Union Congress agreed to the Conservative government's demands that this right to contract out should be made more effective.

A big union has several hundred thousand votes at the conference. It is currently estimated that the individual membership of the constituency parties is hardly any more than 250,000 for the whole U.K. (compared with a million around 1950). So, although the constituency delegations' votes are weighted, the unions have about five-sixths of the total voting weight. Each union's votes are decided by the unions' executives, not their ordinary members. The M.P.s and other affiliated organisations also vote.

In recent years the conference has voted for withdrawal from Europe, unilateral nuclear disarmament, massive new nationalisations, increased trade union power, abolition of the House of Lords and other left-wing policies. It has also required each sitting Labour M.P. to face a contested re-selection process during the life of a Parliament, and changed the rules for choosing the party leader, so that the Labour M.P.s votes have only the same weight in this process as the constituency party delegations, and the unions more weight than either. The new system was first used in 1983, when Neil Kinnock succeeded Michael Foot after the election defeat.

One old Labour Party rule survives: Communist Party members are not eligible for membership—though there are some Communist trade union officials. Lately, however, many local parties have become dominated by left-wingers, including some belonging to a highly organised and disciplined group calling itself 'Militant'.

6 The Working of the House of Commons

Government in Britain is called 'parliamentary government,' but that expression no longer means the same thing as it did a hundred years ago. Then, it was true to say that the ministers held office

The House of Commons, seen from the
Public Gallery
1 Press Gallery
2 Speaker's Chair
3 Opposition front bench
4 Government front bench
5 Dispatch Box
6 Galleries for M.P.s
7 Civil Servants advising ministers
8 Galleries for distinguished visitors, including peers

only for so long as they continued to be supported by a majority in
the House of Commons; now, the possibility that they should be
defeated in the House of Commons is normally so small that the
Government's vulnerability in 1974 and 1977–9 was exceptional.
Nevertheless, the whole system still has its centre in Parliament, and
can only be described through its working Parliament.

The two Houses of Parliament, the Lords and the Commons, share the same building, the Palace of Westminster. The present buildings of the Palace, including the Commons Chamber itself, were badly damaged in an air-raid in 1941, and have been rebuilt since 1945.

The Commons occupy the north part of the Palace, the Lords the south end. The part of the Palace of Westminster used by members and officials of the House of Commons includes some hundreds of rooms, among which are the library, restaurants, committee rooms, and private or shared office rooms for M.P.s.

The Commons debating chamber is only one of the many rooms of the Palace, but is usually called 'the House'. It has seats for only about 370 of its total membership of over 600. The rebuilt chamber is the same size and shape as the old one was, though it has modern air-conditioning, lighting and microphones. Members do not have special seats. On big occasions the chamber is overcrowded, but most of the time the benches provide more than enough room for all the members who are present. The shape and arrangement of the House are of great political significance. It is rectangular, with the Speaker's chair at one end, and with five straight rows of benches running down one side along its whole length, and five rows on the other side, so that the rows of benches face each other across the floor. One side of the House is occupied by the Government and the members who support it, the other, facing them, by Her Majesty's Opposition—all the Members who are opposed to the Government of the day, and who hope that at the next general election their party will be in a majority so that they can form the Government. The arrangement of the benches in the House of Commons suggests a two-party system, and the Leader of the Opposition receives a salary from state funds as if he were a minister.

Members of the House of Commons have been paid salaries since 1911. The rate has lately been nearly twice the average industrial worker's wage. Since 1965 the allowances for travel, living in London, and paying part-time secretaries and research assistants have all been improved. The Library has been extended; its greatly-increased staff help M.P.s to get the information they need for their work. But many M.P.s say that they need to have outside earnings, through journalism, work in the law courts or business, to enable them to live at the standard they expect.

Anyone who is interested in what happens in Parliament can buy a copy of the stenographic record, which is put on sale at big newspaper shops and the shops of Her Majesty's Stationery Office, the government printer. The number of copies sold has fallen very much in the past twenty years. This 'Official Report' is popularly called 'Hansard', because Thomas Hansard started to produce these reports privately in 1803. He began this publication in defiance of a parliamentary rule forbidding any such reporting, but what began as a forbidden venture has become part of Parliament's own services.

Each chamber has galleries, parts of which are kept for the use of the public, who are described, in the language of Parliament, as 'strangers'. It is usually possible to get a seat in the strangers' gallery of the House of Lords at any time, but it is not so easy to get into the House of Commons gallery, particularly in the summer, when London is full of visitors. In order to get a place for the beginning of a day's business at 2.30 p.m., in time for the question hour, it is usually necessary to write in advance to a Member of Parliament for a ticket, though foreign visitors can sometimes get tickets through their embassies. A person who comes without a reservation has usually to wait for a long time, one, two or three hours, until a place becomes free, though very late in the evening it is often possible to get in without waiting.

Standing Orders set out the main formal rules of procedure, but not by any means all the actual rules, many of which are practices established by custom and precedent. In 1844 Sir Thomas Erskine May, who was then Clerk of the House of Commons, published his great *Treatise on the Law, Privileges, Proceedings and Usage of Parliament*. Revised editions of the Treatise have been published from time to time. It is used and followed in other Parliaments of the Commonwealth besides the British. As anyone who reads it can quickly see, very many of the rules are derived from individual decisions of successive Speakers. A Speaker's decision on some particular point may establish a precedent in much the same way as a Court's decision on a matter of law. So the office of the Speaker (or President of the Chamber) has a special importance.

The choice of a new Speaker is made by a vote of the House after the party leaders have consulted their supporters and privately agreed beforehand on a particular person. Once a man has been made Speaker he is customarily reappointed to his office in each new Parliament, even if the majority in the House has changed, until he wishes to retire. When he accepts office as Speaker he is expected to renounce all party politics for the rest of his life; this means that the people of his constituency have no normal partisan representative in Parliament. When he retires he is at once made a peer, and goes to the House of Lords. Three other members hold office as deputy-speakers, and they take turns at occupying the Chair. The three deputies abstain from all party activity for so long as they hold office, but may—and sometimes do—return to ordinary political activity after a time.

The central rule of procedure is that every debate must relate to a specific proposal, or 'motion'. Some Member moves (proposes) a motion; the House debates it and finally decides whether to agree or to disagree with it. A motion may propose that the House should take some action (for example, give a 'second reading' to a bill), or that it should express some opinion. When a motion has been moved, another Member may propose to 'amend' it, and in that case his proposal is debated. When the House has decided on the amendment it goes back to the original motion, which is now in a new form if an amendment to it has been accepted. A debate ends either (1) when every Member who wants to speak has done so, or (2) at a time fixed in advance either by informal agreement between the parties or by a vote of the House (that is, by the Government without the agreement of the Opposition), or (3) when the House, with the Speaker's consent, votes that it shall end.

At the end of every debate the Speaker puts the question whether or not to accept the motion that has been debated. If there is disagreement, there is a 'division' and Members vote by walking through corridors called 'lobbies', being counted as they do so. The names of Members voting are recorded and published. The 'Aye' (yes) lobby runs down one side of the outside wall of the chamber, the 'No' lobby down the other side. Six minutes after the beginning of the division the doors leading into the lobbies are locked. The practice of allowing six minutes before Members must enter their lobbies gives enough time for them to come from any part of the Palace of Westminster. Bells ring all over the building to summon Members to the chamber to vote. Members often vote without having heard a debate, and perhaps without knowing exactly what is the question; they know which way to vote because Whips (or party managers) of the parties stand outside the doors, and Members vote almost automatically with their parties.

The House of Commons meets every Monday, Tuesday,

Wednesday and Thursday at 2.30 in the afternoon, and normally sits until 10.30 p.m., although often it may continue to sit later still—often until eleven or twelve, and occasionally until one or two o'clock in the morning or even all through the night. On Fridays it meets at 9.30 in the morning and finishes at three p.m. A light at the top of the clock tower, where the famous Big Ben strikes, is kept on for so long as the House is sitting.

Many Members go to their constituencies, whether their homes are there or not, during the weekends. They need to see their local party organisers from time to time, and to be available to citizens who wish to discuss grievances or other problems. They also make speeches, not only in their constituencies but in other places too. On Sundays they can try to arrange things so that they can be with their families. But they also have holidays of about four weeks over Christmas, two weeks each at Easter and Whitsun, and about eleven weeks—from early August to mid-October—in the summer.

The life of Parliament is divided into periods called 'sessions'. At the end of every session Parliament is 'prorogued'; this means that all business which has not been completed is abandoned, and Parliament cannot meet again until it is formally summoned by the Queen. Every new session begins with a clean slate. A session normally lasts for about a year, from late October of one year to about the same date of the next year, though if a general election is held in the spring or summer the normal rhythm of the sessions is interrupted.

The beginning of a new session, called 'the State Opening of Parliament', is a fine ceremonial occasion, beginning with the royal carriage procession from Buckingham Palace to the Palace of Westminster. The Household Cavalry are there, also the Lord Great Chamberlain, Gold Stick in Waiting, the Master of the Horse, the Gentlemen at Arms, the Yeomen of the Guard and the Ladies of the Bedchamber, and of course the trumpeters, the crowds along the processional route, and now the television cameras. The ceremony takes place in the House of Lords, with a few leading members of the House of Commons standing crowded together at the end of the chamber opposite to the Throne, within the four walls of the room, but technically outside the 'House of Lords' itself.

The Queen takes her place on the throne and reads out the 'Queen's Speech', which is a document, about a thousand words in length, prepared by the Government, in which the Government gives a summary of the things which it intends to do during the session which is about to begin. The members of the House of Commons then go back to their own chamber, and a member of the Government party proposes that a humble address should be presented to the Queen to thank her for her gracious speech. A debate on this proposal then begins, and lasts for five or six days; it is really a succession of debates on particular aspects of the Government's policy as set out in the Queen's Speech. Usually the Opposition propose to add to the address to the Queen some expressions of regret about some part of the Speech or about some omissions from it; at the end of each debate there may be a vote on the Opposition's amendment. If the Government lost such a vote it would presumably have to resign or ask for a general election.

7 The Parliamentary Day

Except on Fridays, each day's business begins, after prayers and some minor preliminaries which take about five minutes, with 'Question Time'. This is a period of about fifty-five minutes, ending at 3.30 p.m., during which Members may address questions to ministers, which ministers normally answer, although they are not obliged to do so. At 3.30 p.m. any minister who has a statement to make, or any other Member who wishes to make a personal statement, says what he has to say and questions may be asked about the statement; also various other things may be done. Exciting but brief arguments often take place at this moment, and the House is usually rather full.

On any day the miscellaneous items which begin at 3.30 p.m. may take together no time at all, or ten minutes, or perhaps half an hour or an hour. When they are finished, the main business of the day begins, and normally continues until 10 p.m., which under the Standing Orders is the hour at which the business should end; sometimes, however, the House has already decided at 3.30 p.m. to allow the main business to continue after 10 p.m. Then there are various special types of business which may be taken after 10 p.m., even under the Standing Orders; and finally, when everything else is finished, thirty minutes are allowed for any Member to make a speech on some subject 'on the adjournment', and for the appropriate minister to reply to him.

The question hour at the beginning of each day's sitting is the most widely-known and admired procedural device of the British

House of Commons, and it has been imitated—though not exactly—in many other countries. This form of procedure was not created or invented; during the early part of the nineteenth century some Members sometimes addressed questions to ministers and received answers, and gradually the practice became so popular that Standing Orders were introduced to regulate the process and to give questions to ministers a definite place in the daily timetable. Two features of this procedure are mainly responsible for its usefulness and success: the use made of the supplementary question and the shortness of all the questions and answers. From thirty to fifty questions and up to a hundred supplementaries are asked and answered during the hour each day.

Every question must be handed to the officials of the House in writing at least 48 hours before the answer is to be given. The officials transmit the questions very quickly to the ministers who will have to answer them, and the answers are prepared by civil servants. For the sake of convenience, questions are not answered exactly in the order in which they have been asked. An informal rota of ministers is arranged, and each day two or three or more ministers deal in turn with the questions to themselves which have accumulated during the period—normally one or two weeks—since they last had their turns at answering. Thus on a typical day there may be eight questions for the minister who is first to answer, twenty for the second, and so on. The Prime Minister is outside the rota; he answers questions addressed to him (on general policy) at 3.15 p.m. on two days a week.

All the questions for answer on a particular day are printed, together with the names of the interrogators, on the day's programme-sheet (called the 'Order Paper'), and each question has a serial number. The Speaker begins the proceedings by calling out the name of the Member who is to ask the first question, and that Member simply stands and says 'Question No. 1'. The minister to whom it is addressed then reads out the reply (or, possibly, gives the reply without reading). Then the Member who asked the question may ask a 'supplementary' question asking for further elucidation, and the minister is expected to reply at once to that also; he and his civil servants have tried to foresee all possible supplementaries, and to be ready with answers. Then other Members may also ask further supplementary questions, and so on until the Speaker decides that it is time to go on to the next question on the paper. He does this by calling out the name of the

Member who is to ask Question No.2. The Speaker has to try to keep down the number of supplementaries enough to allow a reasonable number of questions to be dealt with, but not so much that ministers are excessively protected against awkward supplementaries. This is a very difficult task.

It is not at all easy to classify or analyse parliamentary questions. Some are asked for the purpose of embarrassing the Government, some in order to try to persuade ministers to adopt new courses of action, either in dealing with individual cases or in their general policies. Certainly everybody knows that if any official anywhere in the administration does anything stupid or harsh, it is quite likely that the person aggrieved will write to his Member of Parliament, who will first write or talk to the minister privately about the case, and then, if it seems that justice has not been done, ask a question in all the publicity of the House of Commons. So question time is not only interesting, besides often being a good opportunity for the display of skill and wit; it also helps in a very positive way to prevent the administrative machine from working without due humanity.

If a Member is dissatisfied with a minister's answers, it is quite easy for him to raise the subject again, at greater length, not by putting down another question for a later day but by putting down his name to speak about it during the final half-hour 'debate on the adjournment' at the end of some future day's business. Then he will have time to develop his complaints more thoroughly; but he will have the disadvantage that there will probably be only a few Members present to listen to him. If there is a really serious scandal, and there is real urgency about the matter, he may even be able to make use of the procedure which allows the planned order of business to be changed so as to allow about three hours to be spent at once, or on the next day, in debating something that must be debated quickly if at all. This procedure was for a time much restricted, but has now been made less difficult.

There are always more questions asked by members of the Opposition party than by supporters of the Government. Ministers do not address questions to their own colleagues, but it is commonly accepted that a member of the Government's party who does not hold any office ought not to hesitate to ask a question, even if it will be embarrassing to his own minister, if he thinks that there is good reason to ask it. In fact, there are always some Members on the Government benches who are readier to ask awkward questions than the majority of their colleagues. The House of Commons, like any group, always includes some personalities on both sides who are more forward than the average; it seems that in general some fifty or sixty Members together ask about half of all the questions, while 200 others hardly ever ask any at all.

After question time and the short items of business which sometimes follow it, the House of Commons goes on to the main debate of the day, to which it can usually give about six hours. Sometimes there are two or three short debates in succession, but usually one debate lasts for the whole of the time available.

In a typical session lasting one year the House sits on about 160 days. On twenty-four of these days the subject of discussion is chosen by 'private Members'—that is by individuals, neither the Government nor the Opposition; twenty-eight days must be given nominally to discussing the Government's requests for authority to spend money—though in fact these twenty-eight days are really days on which the Opposition chooses the subject of debate; about six to ten days are needed for discussion of taxation, six, as we have seen, for the debate on the Queen's Speech, and a further fifteen or twenty days for a great variety of matters which have to be fitted into the year's programme. There remain, usually about sixty days for discussion of the bills (proposals for new laws or changes in old laws) which the Government wants to have passed.

There is no formal steering committee to arrange the order of business; except on the twenty-four 'private Members' days' which are now allowed in each session, the decision how the time is to be allocated is made at private and informal meetings between the Chief Whips, or party managers, of the Government and Opposition parties. Each Thursday at 3.30 p.m. or a little later, the Leader of the House (always a prominent minister) announces the programme of business for the following week, and although Members may then complain briefly about the shape of the programme, they make their complaints mainly in order to get publicity for their own ideas which are not to be debated.

On a typical day the main debate lasts from about 3.45 or 4 p.m. until 10 p.m. It is opened by a minister or by an Opposition spokesman, as the case may be. If the first speaker is a member of the Government, it is most probably the minister in charge of the department immediately concerned with the topic which is to be discussed. He speaks from the place on the Government front bench which is opposite the 'dispatch box'—a kind of reading-desk on the long table which stands in front of the Speaker and between the two front benches. The minister thus faces the Opposition and has his back towards his own supporters. His speech will probably last for thirty or forty minutes, or perhaps even longer. When he has finished, the Opposition spokesman makes his speech, of about the same length, from the place in front of the similar dispatch box which stands on the Opposition side of the table. Afterwards the debate is continued by ordinary Members (collectively called 'unofficial' or 'private' Members, or sometimes 'back-benchers') until a time, probably nine o'clock, at which it will have been agreed that a second Opposition spokesman will begin a speech to wind up the debate for his party. Then at 9.30 p.m. a second Government spokesman will have his turn and when he has finished the debate is ended.

There are thus about four hours on such a typical day, from about five until nine in the evening, during which back-benchers may make their speeches. The average speech lasts for about fifteen minutes (though there is no formal time limit), so about fifteen Members are able to speak in a typical debate. They speak as they are called upon by the Speaker or Deputy-Speaker, who always calls upon Members from the two sides of the House alternately, so far as possible. There is no predetermined order of speaking; as soon as a Member on the Government side has finished, all the Opposition Members who want to intervene stand up in the hope of being called, and the Speaker calls on one of them. He has absolute discretion in his choice. He may give preference to a Member he knows to have special knowledge of the subject under discussion, or to one who represents some particular minority opinion. A new Member who has never spoken before is always given priority.

This lack of plan about the order of speaking is often criticised, because it causes so many Members to come to the House with speeches specially prepared, only to find the debate ending without their ever having been called upon to speak; but in general it is felt that by this means spontaneity is best preserved.

Interruptions during speeches are quite frequent. If a Member making a speech sees another stand up, he may sit down and allow a brief interruption. He is not obliged to give way, but his reputation will suffer if he obstinately refuses to do so.

8 How Laws are Passed

The British Parliament, like parliaments in other countries, is often referred to as 'the Legislature'—the body which makes laws. Its essential function could probably be best described as 'to discuss what the Government has done, is doing and intends to do, and on occasion to try to show up the Government's errors and even try to persuade the Government to change or modify its policies'. Nevertheless, new laws can only come into force when they have passed through Parliament, and the way in which it deals with bills (that is, proposals for new laws) gives a good illustration of Parliament's working.

Most bills, and nearly all important bills, are introduced by the Government. About fifty bills are passed each year, some of them short and uncontroversial, some of them long and needing much discussion—though the importance of a bill is not necessarily indicated by its length. Every bill brought in by the Government has been approved first by the Cabinet; in fact, in any year, there are nearly always more bills which the Government would like to have passed than it can find time to put through Parliament.

Once the Government has decided to introduce a bill, one minister is put in charge of it. The preparation of the text may take many months, with long consultations involving civil servants in the minister's department on the one hand and Parliamentary Counsel on the other. (These are a small group of legal experts who are concerned with the technical side of the drafting, or writing, of bills. All the laws in force are collected together in the 'book' of statutes, in which each law is a 'chapter'. Acts of Parliament have to be interpreted by the Courts, and every law must conform to the special usages and interpretations of the statute book.) At the same time, the civil servants will probably have conferences with officials from other departments, and also with representatives of groups of people (such as associations of traders or manufacturers or workers or dentists or cyclists, or people who keep bees) who may be affected or interested in some way by the proposed new law.

At last the bill is ready to be submitted to Parliament. It will have to be passed by both Houses of Parliament, one after the other. It can begin its journey in either the House of Commons or the House of Lords, though all really important or controversial bills are in fact submitted to the House of Commons first.

A typical bill of moderate importance, then, will begin in the House of Commons. According to very ancient practice, it must have three 'readings' there, although the use of this word is a little misleading. The 'first reading' is in effect merely an announcement that the bill is coming forward. After the first reading the printed text of the bill is published. After the text has been in circulation for a reasonable length of time (usually one or two weeks at least), some time, say a whole day, is provided in the timetable of the House of Commons for the debate on the 'second reading'. This is the main debate on the general principles and objectives of the bill, and at the end of the debate a vote is taken; if the Opposition do not like it they will vote against it. A vote on the second reading of a Government bill is, like almost all votes in the House of Commons, an occasion when the members of the two main parties vote in blocks, with few deviations. The important thing about this stage is not the final decision, but the words spoken in the debate, the arguments for and against, the discussion of principles and of details from many points of view. A Government supporter may make a speech in which he criticises a bill and then vote for it, but his words may have some effect.

After passing the second reading stage the bill must then go to a committee for detailed examination, in the course of which there may be many proposals for amendment. The committee stage of a bill affecting the Constitution (such as devolution of powers to Scotland or elections to the European Parliament) is taken in a Committee of the whole House, in the Commons chamber but with the Speaker absent; but most bills are sent to small 'standing' committees for the discussion of details. The House can set up as many standing committees as are needed, but the number is usually not more than five. The committees are not specialised, and are not really 'standing' or permanent at all. There is a new committe for each bill. Any bill relating only to Scotland is sent to a committee composed entirely of Members who represent constituencies in Scotland. In practice there is one standing committee which deals with bills proposed by ordinary Members; all the others deal with bills proposed by ministers. For major bills the committee contains forty-five members, though the number may be less, and for uncontroversial bills is often only thirty-five or less.

The committee places are distributed among the parties according to their relative numerical strength in the House, so, assuming that the Government has a majority in the House, it has also a majority in each standing committee. Standing committees normally meet on Tuesdays and Thursdays in the morning, in rooms each designed like a miniature House of Commons. The minister who is in charge of the bill and the Member who is leading for the Opposition sit opposite to one another on the front benches just as the main party spokesmen do in the House.

The function of the committee on a bill is to go through the text in detail, and possibly to make changes in it. Any member of the committee may propose to alter the text, by inserting new words or by omitting words which are in the original text, or by substituting new words. His proposal to change (or 'amend') the text is discussed, and then the committee decides whether or not to make the amendment which he proposes. Proposals for amendment are normally given to officials in writing some days before the committee meets, and they are then printed, arranged in the order in which they come in relation to the original text of the bill.

Whenever an amendment is proposed, the minister either agrees to accept it or refuses, or asks for it to be withdrawn so that there may be some private discussion about it. If he refuses, there may be a vote, but the minister's party people always vote for him, and he is sure of having a majority. Ministers do in fact very often accept proposals for amendment, either in their original form or in some form which is agreed to as a compromise.

Committee proceedings on a single bill may take two mornings a week for two to ten or even fifteen weeks, with dozens of proposals for amendment debated one after another. A debate may be closured by a majority vote if the chairman (who acts impartially) thinks the debate has been long enough. Long and controversial bills are usually 'guillotined', with debate subject to a detailed time limit.

The committee stage of a bill illustrates very clearly the position of organised groups of people who have particular interests in relation to the political process. Most proposals for amendment of a bill are suggested to committee members by associations which think that their interests are threatened, or not helped, by the bill as it has been brought in by the Government. They may already have presented their arguments to the minister or his civil servants privately beforehand, and their suggestions may then have been refused; in that case the committee discussion gives an opportunity to a Member of Parliament, acting as their spokesman, to oblige the minister to think again, perhaps to make a concession, or at least to make a public defence of his reasons for not giving them what they want.

After the committee has finished with a bill, the next stage is called 'the Report stage'. The House itself now repeats the committee stage, though taking much less time. The House has before it the new text of the bill, incorporating the committee's amendments. Some new amendments are proposed; there may be further discussion of the amendments which were proposed in committee but withdrawn there so as to give the minister time to examine them thoroughly—and these are now decided upon, or withdrawn again, perhaps in the hope that after even more discussion the minister will be ready to tell the Government spokesman to accept them in the House of Lords.

The last stage is the debate on the proposal to 'read the bill a third time'. This debate is usually fairly short. It is a final review and discussion of the bill as it stands after amendment.

Next the bill must go through the same stages in the House of Lords. If the House of Lords should reject a bill which has been passed by the Commons, the bill can go no further for a few months; but if the Commons pass it again, in substantially the same form as before, it must go to the Queen for her signature no matter what the Lords do. The position of the House of Lords will be discussed in a later chapter; now it can be said that, as the Lords seem unlikely to reject a bill proposed by the Government, the real importance of the passage through the House of Lords is in the Committee stage there.

Normally, when a Government has an overall majority in the Commons, Parliament is not acting as a pure Legislature, or law-making body, but as a forum in which ministers hear arguments about their own proposals and impose their own decisions. But there is also some opportunity for Parliament to act as a true Legislature, when it deals with bills proposed by its own back-bench members. Every M.P. may introduce a bill at any time. Several dozens of bills are proposed every year but make no progress because no time is provided for their debate. But about eight Fridays a year are allocated for second reading debates on bills proposed by ordinary M.P.s ('private Members' bills'), and eight more Fridays for the later stages of such bills which have passed second reading and committee. Priority on these private Members' Fridays is allocated by a ballot.

Private Members' bills usually deal with matters about which Governments do not wish to legislate because they involve personal conscience or private behaviour. Votes are free; but with the Whips not giving any instructions M.P.s often go off to their constituencies on private Members' Fridays, so the attendance is often small. Nevertheless, since 1965 several important reforms have been introduced in this way, including the abolition of the death penalty. The laws about divorce, abortion and censorship of obscenity, have been liberalised. Parliament is a little strengthened when it can take such decisions by its own free majority. In most years about ten private Members' bills are enacted into law.

Since 1972 Parliament has been allowed a real legislative role in relation to some important constitutional reforms, beginning with Europe. In 1972 the Conservative Government allowed free votes in the bill providing for Britain's entry to the European Community; and so did the Labour Government on the bill providing for the referendum of 1975 and in 1977 for the elections to the European Parliament. There were free votes too on the proposals for devolution for Scotland and Wales in 1976–8. And in 1974 and again in 1977–8, with a minority government in office, the whole pattern of governmental domination over Parliament was modified. But these instances of parliamentary power must be regarded as exceptions to a general trend which seems likely in the long run to be reversed only if a future government is based on a minority party; and that is unlikely unless the electoral system is changed.

9 Control of Government Expenditure, Taxation and Administration

Parliament has other things to do as well as pass bills. The Government cannot legally spend any money without the permission of the House of Commons. This permission is given in the form of Acts of Parliament authorising the payment of sums of money out of the consolidated fund, which can be regarded as the Government's central bank account.

Before the annual Appropriation Bill is passed the House votes on some two hundred items of expenditure, but this is done in a few minutes. However, the right to control expenditure is recognised by a convention that twenty-eight days each year must be guaranteed as 'supply' days, or days on which estimates of expenditure may be discussed. On these days (nearly one per week, on average) the Opposition choose the subjects of debate; they are normally used to debate policy, rather than the detailed plans for expenditure. The ancient procedure was simplified in 1967. Only the Government is allowed to propose expenditure, but each year there is a debate on a document which shows what the Government expects to spend on each main item in each of the next five years. These plans are only tentative, so M.P.s may advocate increases as well as decreases; a vote on the forward plan has no real effect.

In abandoning the attempt to discuss the details of expenditure in 'Committee of Supply', the House of Commons has shown much realism. Recognising that Government policy is party policy, which the voters have approved by giving the party a majority at the last general election, the House of Commons leaves the expert officials of the departments and the Treasury to decide how much it will cost to carry out the policies. The House still discusses the merits of the policies, but does not try to discuss the cost. It does, however, establish two small committees of its own members.

The House of Commons still keeps a rather closer contact with taxation. Each year the taxes are authorised by a Finance Act, which is based on the Budget presented by the Chancellor of the Exchequer in April. In the detailed discussions members try to persuade the Chancellor to reduce particular taxes, and they are not always unsuccessful.

The House of Commons spends many more hours in session each year than any other parliamentary assembly, but for most of the time less than fifty M.P.s are present listening to the one who is speaking.

About one-seventh of this time is taken by senior and junior ministers stating the Government's policy or replying to questions and arguments put by the Opposition or by back-benchers of all parties. Rather less time is taken by Opposition front-bench spokesman. The rest, about three-quarters, is occupied by back-benchers of the Government and Opposition parties, though in 1974–8 spokesmen for the minor parties made a more than average contribution.

During any year almost every corner of the nation's business is dealt with in debate. The average back-bencher makes about four 15-minute speeches in a year, usually to a nearly empty chamber, though he is heard by ministers from the department responsible for the matter about which he is speaking. Most back-benchers' speeches are based on material supplied by national or local interests, and a large proportion deal with matters of concern to the M.P.'s own constituents. Back-bench speeches hardly ever influence the voting, though ministers may be impressed by what they hear, and sometimes modify their policies accordingly. Most back-benchers' arguments have already been put before departments through other contacts outside Parliament, or in private Party committees; but the fact that they are put in open debate obliges the minister to listen and react.

For a long time it was argued that the House of Commons ought to have a system of committees, corresponding with the main government departments. After a series of experiments over many years (some of them very successful), a system of this kind was at last created in 1979–80.

Each of these select committees has a more or less permanent membership, so that it can develop a thorough knowledge of the general problems associated with the work of its department. There are special advisers from outside Parliament, and individual members may employ their own research assistants. When a committee decides on a particular investigation, its clerk asks the department for a memorandum and statistics, and civil servants are called before the committee to answer questions. People from outside the administration may also be called in. The question sessions are held in public, and a stenographic record of the proceedings is published. Finally, the committee prepares and publishes a report, which most probably suggests changes in the way things have been done. Some reports are discussed in the press or debated in the House, and some have some real influence—partly because committee-members usually forget about party for this work. But in his constituency an M.P. gets more reward for ideological vigour than for less glamorous work in a committee.

10 The Future of British Politics

Several senior Labour politicians left the party in the 1970s, dismayed by its leftward drift. The former Deputy-Leader Roy Jenkins, who had also been Foreign Secretary, Home Secretary and Chancellor of the Exchequer, left Parliament when he became President of the European Commission, and soon after he returned in 1980 was joined by three other leading Labour moderates in forming a wholly new party, the Social Democrats.

Soon more than 22 M.P.s, some peers and moderate activists joined them in leaving the Labour Party and setting up a nation-wide organisation, which also attracted a few moderate

Conservatives and many people who had until then not been in any party. The new group formed an alliance with the Liberals. Before long these two bodies, still separate, ran into difficulties over decisions as to which would fight which seats at the next election, and publicity given to these rifts may have helped to reduce the Alliance's public following, as indicated by opinion polls, from the highest figure it briefly attained—about half of the electorate in 1981—to around a quarter in the next three years.

A study of the voting trends through several elections could well suggest that the two-party system is in decline—and opinion polls have regularly indicated huge majorities disliking both the trade unions' role and power and Labour's leftist policies (except withdrawal from Europe). But the scale of Labour's electoral disaster in 1983, when the percentage Labour vote per Labour candidate was lower than in any election since the party's foundation in 1900, seemed to shock the left wing into silence. The new leader, Neil Kinnock, had been identified with the party's left but not its 'hard left', and outside Parliament the newly proclaimed party unity seemed based on a new moderation. In the next year Labour's popular support grew, while that for the Alliance did not.

For almost every British person able to vote in 1987, voting has always meant a choice between left and right, Conservative and Labour. That choice has been heavily based on class. Around two-thirds of people considering themselves working class have mostly voted Labour, though the proportions have been higher among those living in council houses and/or working in coalmines and large scale industry. Among white collar workers, very few of whom live in council houses, rather more than two-thirds have mostly voted Conservative—though the proportion varies with grade of job, and preference for Labour is relatively high among those working in the public sector, particularly teachers.

Since 1970 these categories have been modified by a decrease in attachment to both major parties. At least half of the existing electorate have changed their party preference at some time, some moving only between Conservative and Labour, many occasionally supporting Liberals—and lately the Alliance. Of those who vote Conservative, many are really concerned mainly to keep Labour out, and vice versa. The impact of the Alliance at an election in 1987 or 1988 must depend on two factors: first, obviously, the size of its support; second the size of the gap in seats between the major parties. To win a substantial number of seats under the existing electoral system (which is unlikely to be changed before then) the Alliance needs more than one-third of the votes, and there is not much probability that it will get them. Two special Liberal plans (apart from Proportional Representation) are for regional government, which arouses no interest, and for co-partnership in industry, which the public may see as good in principle, but impracticable. With little else specific to offer, the Alliance cannot be well placed to prevent the two-party system from maintaining itself for a long time yet.

Taxes[1] as percentages of gross national product at factor cost: international comparison, 1980				
		percentages		
	Direct	Indirect	Social security	Total
Norway	25	20	14	59
Sweden	24	15	16	55
Netherlands	18	14	20	52
Austria	15	19	15	49
France	10	17	21	48
Belgium	21	13	14	48
Germany (Fed. Rep.)	14	14	16	44
United Kingdom	17	18	7	42
Finland	17	17	5	39
Italy	12	12	14	38
Irish Republic	13	17	7	36
Canada	18	14	4	36
Australia	20	15	0	35
USA	16	9	8	33
Greece	7	15	10	32
Switzerland	15	7	9	31
Japan	12	8	8	28
Spain[2]	6	7	13	26

[1] All central government, state, and local government taxes, and social security contributions.
[2] Data relate to 1979.

Question

Does high public expenditure from taxation relate to the level of overall production in a country?

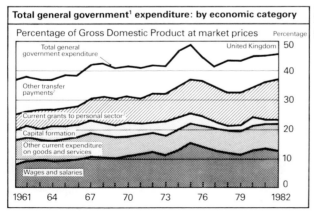

Total general government[1] expenditure: by economic category

Percentage of Gross Domestic Product at market prices   Percentage

Total general government expenditure

United Kingdom   50

40

Other transfer payments[2]

30

Current grants to personal sector[3]

20

Capital formation

Other current expenditure on goods and services

10

Wages and salaries

0

1961   64   67   70   73   76   79   1982

[1] Combined central government and local authority sector
[2] Mainly subsidies, debt interest, other central government and local authority grants, and loans
[3] Social security payments, educational grants, etc.

Question

What does this table tell us about the difficulties faced by a government seeking to reduce public expenditure?

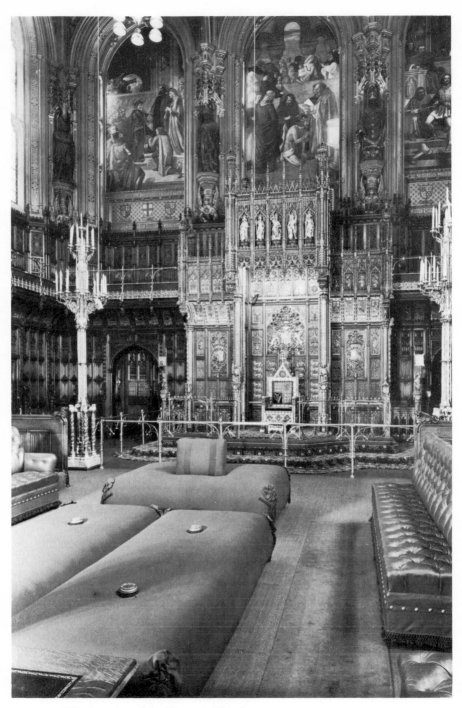

The interior of the House of Lords.

3

The House of Lords

1   Will the House of Lords survive?

Britain is unique in keeping a second house of Parliament with a
mainly hereditary membership. Hardly anyone seriously defends
this survival from the past, but attempts at fundamental reform
have been frustrated by disagreements about proposed solutions.
One change, allowing women to be included, was made in 1958,
against the sole objections of an 83 year-old eighth holder of an
earldom going back to 1703. To be a member you must either
inherit a peerage, from father or ancestor, or have a peerage
conferred on you by the Queen, on the Prime Minister's advice.
The numbers are not fixed, and have increased up to the present
total of around 1,200. Of these, nearly 800 have inherited their
peerages, while about 400 have had peerages conferred on them,
including about 50 women.

A body with such a composition cannot feel justified in
exercising real power in a modern state. Since the 1949 Parliament
Act the House of Lords had had only a power to delay the
enactment of a new law from one session of Parliament to the next,
and it has not intentionally used even this power. There is also one
special power of absolute veto, if the House of Commons should
pass a bill to extend its own life, without a new general election,
beyond five years from the previous election. The Lords could have
used this power in 1915 and 1940, but did not do so, because all
parties agreed that a general election in wartime would be
inconvenient.

The House of Lords is the continuation into modern times of the
original Norman King's Court, to which the King summoned the
great men of the land. Each was summoned individually, and the
right to be summoned passed to the eldest son. Later the right was
associated with the grant of a specific hereditary title (lord). From

time to time new peerages were conferred. Some soon became extinct through the lack of any heir, others survived through many generations. In 1976 the 16th Duke of Norfolk died, and was succeeded by the 17th Duke, as holder of a dukedom dating back to 1483—and this was not as old as the barony of Lord Mowbray (1283).

The House of Lords was abolished in 1649, by resolution of Cromwell's House of Commons ('the House of Lords is useless and dangerous and ought to be abolished'). With the restoration of the monarchy in 1660 the old House of Lords was restored too, and it resumed its existence as though nothing had happened. Soon the Commons insisted that the Lords should not concern themselves with taxation or expenditure, and the Lords acquiesced until 1909, when an attempt at interference led to a reduction of their powers. Otherwise there was little formal change until the Life Peerages Act of 1958 (allowing non-hereditary peerages to be conferred) and the Peerage Act of 1962, enabling a peer to renounce his peerage and so to become eligible, as a 'Mr', for election to the Commons, where all serious politics happen. The first to renounce his title was the second Lord Stansgate, who was soon re-elected to the Commons as Tony Benn; he was soon followed by the 14th Earl of Home, who became Conservative Prime Minister in 1963 as Sir Alec Douglas-Home.

Fundamentally the system has never changed, though from the eighteenth century all new peerages have been given on the Prime Minister's advice. Two survivals from the past are the inclusion of the 26 senior bishops of the Church of England, and the function of the House of Lords as the highest court of appeal in the judicial system. However, its work as a court of law is effectively quite separate from its functions as part of the Legislature. The nine appeal judges now hold non-hereditary peerages of a special kind, based on a law of 1876. They occasionally speak on legal issues, and the bishops on social problems, but both these groups now tend to avoid getting embroiled in partisan politics.

Until about 1700 new peerages were given very sparingly, and at that time there were only 70 temporal peers. Gradually the number of new peerages conferred increased, and in the nineteenth century most M.P.'s who had been ministers in the Cabinet received peerages when they retired. So, too, did the biggest industrialists and a few generals and public officers. Until 1958 every newly-created temporal peer was succeeded by his eldest son, and then by succeeding generations; so the membership of the House of Lords increased beyond a thousand. By 1958 there were 800 holders of inherited peerages.About half of these peerages were less than a hundred years old, but most of their holders owned estates in the country, and were easily assimilated with the older aristocracy.

Since the Life Peerage Act of 1958, about 15 to 30 new peers have been added to the House of Lords each year, all on the Prime Minister's recommendation; but each Prime Minister has included, not only his own party men and women, but people suggested by the Opposition and Liberal leaders, trade union officials and a greatly increased number of non-political people with experience of widely differing aspects of business and social affairs.

There are now about 400 life peers, including about 50 women. The exact members are constantly changing. The number has increased until the mid-1980s but will stabilise at around this figure if new additions do not exceed deaths, which will now rise. As it is rare for a person to be given a life peerage before the age of 55, and there is no provision for retirement, the average age is 68, including some who are so old that they hardly or never attend. Out of the total membership of over 1100 peers, about 700 attend at least once a year. Most of these are Conservatives, but only about 300 individuals (mainly life peers) might be considered as more or less regular attenders, and the party balance in the working house is not unlike that of the British voters at the 1983 election: about two-fifths Conservatives, just over a quarter Labour, the rest a mixture of Liberals, Social Democrats and people with no attachment to any party. The number attending varies widely between 200 and 400 from day to day, depending on the programme of business. All active party peers may attend informal weekly meetings of their groups, and receive their party Whip, a document setting out future programmes of business and requesting attendance for important votes. The peers appointed as party Whips discuss the arrangement of business with their own supporters, and the programme is prepared after discussion between government and other Whips. Even the non-party peers have a 'Whip' organisation for this purpose.

The House of Lords is at its best in its debates without vote, at least once a week, on topics of general current interest. In the course of a year the House hears most of the greatest acknowledged experts in the country speaking on their own topics. Ministers and civil servants may listen, or read the speeches in the stenographic record (Lords' *Hansard*), and may be influenced; as they may be too by a letter to *The Times* (which may be even more influential). A good speech in the Lords may lead to an invitation to contribute to a discussion on television; it is all part of the process of public discussion, inside and outside Parliament. So too is the work of the Lords' sub-committees on aspects of European Community legislation.

But the Lords' main work is on the detailed consideration of government bills. Every bill must pass both Houses, but the Lords' power is defined by the Parliament Acts of 1911 and 1949. If the Lords reject a bill which the Commons have passed, the bill can go for the Royal assent if passed by the Commons again in the next session of Parliament. The same applies if the Houses fail to agree on the details of the bill. In fact the House of Lords almost never used this limited power in the 35 years from 1949.

The Lords consider every bill in detail, and make many hundreds of amendments to bills in every year. Whatever the government in power, many of these amendments are proposed by the government, or willingly accepted by it, usually as some kind of compromise. But many other proposals to amend bills are controversial and decided by vote, mainly on party lines.

It has often been said that as the House of Lords has a Conservative majority among its total membership, it is a serious obstacle to a government of the left, but compliant and useless under a Conservative government. Lately the reverse has been true.

When Labour was in office in 1964–70 and 1974–79, the Lords made several hundreds of deletions, additions or other changes to government bills by vote, against the government's wishes. Nearly all of these were later cancelled by the Commons, after short debates, and the Lords accepted the Commons' decisions. In 1970–74 and since 1979 the Conservative governments have indeed won most of the votes on controversial proposals to amend their bills. But sometimes they have been defeated (40 times in 1979–83), usually by a combination of Labour, Liberal and non-party peers, and have been much more ready than Labour to accept defeat in the Lords.

Labour's difficulties with the Lords produced furious complaints about intolerable interference by an undemocratic body with the supposed will of the people as expressed by the government in office. But the Conservatives' respect for the House of Lords, even with its admittedly absurd composition, led them to be much more tolerant of its interference, and thus give it increased real effectiveness.

The Thatcher government's respectful attitude to the House of Lords agreed with the party's 1979 manifesto statement that 'a strong second chamber is necessary not only to revise legislation but also to guarantee our constitution and liberties'. Before the election a party committee, led by Lord Home, had proposed that a sizeable new element, elected by proportional representation, should be added to the second chamber, in order to give it the real legitimacy needed to make it strong. But the question was soon submerged by other issues, and no action has been taken.

The existing House of Lords performs its functions very well, though it has almost no real powers and does not use even the power of delay which it has under the Parliament Acts. The Labour Party's wish to abolish it (stated in the 1983 election manifesto) appears to be supported by only about one-sixth of the population, though a majority would like it to be at least partly elected (cf a Marplan poll, published in the *Guardian*, 23rd July 1983). Elected members of a second chamber would obviously have a more democratically acceptable claim to exercise real power than the members of the present House, who all owe their seats in it either to inheritance or a prime minister's patronage. Mrs Thatcher may be readier than the Labour Party to accept the small inconveniences caused to a government by the present feeble House of Lords, but even she might not wish to face a rival to the Commons endowed with real confidence in its legitimacy.

2 Titles and Honours

British titles are complicated and confusing, because of their long history. When a man or woman is made a peer he or she may choose to continue to use the family name for the title, or alternatively take a place-name. Former Prime Minister Attlee became Earl Attlee, but Eden became Earl of Avon, Avon being the river flowing past the town of Warwick, which he had represented in the House of Commons. If the family name is used, it must have added to it the words '(of some place)', and if there are two or more lords with the same name as their title, this additional name is generally used so as to avoid confusion.

In 1970 George Brown was given a peerage. He had earlier been deputy-leader of the Labour Party and Foreign Secretary, and M.P.

for Belper since 1945. There was already a Lord Brown, and a Lord Belper, so he could not be called by either of those names, and it would have been rather dull to be called Lord Brown of Belper. He would have liked to be called Lord George Brown, but 'Lord (or Lady)—Christian name—Surname' is a style reserved for the younger sons (or daughters) of dukes and marquesses, who are not members of the House of Lords. So he found a marvellous compromise: Lord George-Brown. It was accepted.

Peerages form only a small part of the intricate system of British honours. Every year about 150 men are made knights, in one of seven Orders which are graded in prestige. A knight is called 'Sir—Christian name—Surname' (e.g. Sir Laurence Olivier or more familiarly 'Sir Laurence' or even just 'Olivier', but never 'Sir Olivier'), and his wife is called 'Lady' instead of 'Mrs', though with the wife the Christian name is not used—e.g. Lady Olivier. The title of Dame of the British Empire is a female equivalent to knighthood, but even now there are only about 250 Dames compared with 3,000 Knights. Knights and Dames remain commoners and have no special privileges apart from the title, and their sons are plain 'Mr's. Their titles are not hereditary.

Honours lists are published twice a year under the Prime Minister's responsibility, though the real work of choosing people is done by a network of officials, who ensure a liberal distribution of knighthoods and lesser honours to civil servants and the armed forces according to their rank. There are several Orders, of which people may be made Knights or merely Commanders, Companions or Members. The largest is the Order of the British Empire, and the graded distinctions of C.B.E., O.B.E. and M.B.E. are distributed to hundreds of worthy citizens who are judged to have done good work either in their jobs or in voluntary organisations. Equivalent grades, including knighthoods, in the more prestigious orders of the Bath, St. Michael and St. George, etc. are given to civil servants according to abstruse rules.

British people are by no means indifferent to all these titles and honours. The letters after people's names are always used in lists of directors of companies or of patrons of good causes; the presence of names with titles or letters after them is considered to enhance the prestige of a company or other body. A few men, particularly those whose political views are to the Left, say that they are indifferent to all these titles, and even that they despise them. The recipients of titles and other awards enjoy the process of receiving them; they generally go to Buckingham Palace to receive them at the hands of the Queen at a ceremony known as an investiture. Thus the honours conferred by the state share some of the mysterious magic of royalty, which still holds most British people under its spell.

Types of members of the House of Lords (mid 1983)		
	men	women
Inherited peerages	768	18
'Created' hereditary peers	32	—
Life peers (1958 Act)	286	44
Legal life peers (1876 Act)	20	—
Archbishops and bishops (while in office)	26	—
Total	1122	62

Question

Does the survival of the House of Lords tell us something useful about the nature of British politics?

The Town Hall at Hemel Hempstead in Hertfordshire.

4

Local Government

1   The Permanent Principles

Although the United Kingdom is a unitary state, not a federal one, a very large part of the public services are administered by local authorities, which together employ more than two million people. The central government employs only one-third as many. Scotland and Northern Ireland have their own systems, which are not quite the same as that of England and Wales, though the differences are only superficial. For the sake of simplicity, this chapter will deal only with England and Wales.

All local authorities derive their existence and their powers and functions from Parliament and the central government. Parliament can take powers away or add to them, and it can even abolish any particular authority, or group or class of authorities, if it wants to. But it is inclined to try to respect arrangements regarded as traditional, even when it makes changes in the interest of efficiency. The Local Government Act of 1972 completely reorganised the whole system, bringing a new structure into effect in April 1974.

Although the central Parliament has these powers of life and death over local authorities, and has used them recently, it has never exercised any detailed supervision through any office of the nature of prefect or local governor. Many of the activities of local authorities are in fact supervised, advised or controlled by the central government, but there is no single agency of control for any particular local authority or class of authorities. In each area the elected council and its offices have direct relations with the various central government departments—though these may have regional offices through which some of the central-local relations are conducted.

Traditionally, the most important local area is the county. England has been divided into counties for more than 1,000 years, though in very early times the counties were called 'shires', and most counties, like Yorkshire, still have 'shire' as part of their names. The 40 old English counties vary greatly in size and population. The smallest in population, Rutland, has 20,000 inhabitants; the biggest, Lancashire, has 5,000,000.

At various dates between 1100 and 1970 nearly all large and medium-sized towns were given their own charters of incorporation, either as 'boroughs' or as 'cities'. The title of 'city' has no real significance; it is merely a title of distinction given at some time as a sign of a town's special importance.

Parishes are local communities based on churches. Outside towns the people of parishes elect parish councils, which have some very small functions in relation to local government and local welfare. In towns the parishes lost all their local government functions in the nineteenth century, remaining only as units of church organisation when new civil authorities were created.

In the 1880s large towns (with more than 50,000 inhabitants) were given independent status for local government, as 'county boroughs', and from then until 1974 a county borough council was the only authority for its area, quite separate from the geographical county within whose territory it was situated. Outside the big towns the county councils were responsible for large-scale functions, such as education and the police, but each county was subdivided into second-tier authority-zones of three types—non-county boroughs, urban districts and rural districts. A fairly small town which had been given status as a borough, or even as a city, at some time in the past, kept that status but was responsible only for some local government functions. Other small towns, which had never been given status as boroughs, were designated as 'urban districts', with fewer functions than the non-county boroughs. Outside the towns, each county was divided into rural districts, and the rural district councils were responsible for minor functions.

In the mid-twentieth century the system established in the 1880s was unsatisfactory in many ways. Towns spread out their suburbs far beyond the administrative limits that had been drawn at that time, but attempts to extend the administrative boundaries always produced fierce opposition. By the 1950s many rural districts included big urban and suburban areas, and the distinction between town and country was much less clear than it had been. Planning became difficult, and much of the organisation was irrational. The irrationality was worst of all in the 'conurbations'.

2 The Reforms in London, 1965–84

The first recent change in local government affected London. An
Act of Parliament was passed in 1963 and the new system came into
effect in 1965. Eighty years before, a county of London had been
created, including an area larger than that of the City of Paris, but
less than that of the old Dèpartement de la Seine. By 1921 the
County of London had 4½ million inhabitants, but the suburbs had
already encroached on the four counties surrounding it. In 1921–61,
between census dates, there were two new developments. More and
more people moved into the London area, but some of them and of
the old inhabitants moved to new houses further and further from
the centre. The old East End lost more than half of its population.
By 1961 there were more people living in the ring of continuous
urban development surrounding the County of London than there
were within the County. Planning of all kinds was made difficult
by the lack of an overall authority.

The London Government Act of 1963 created a new county of
Greater London, which came into existence in 1965. Its limits
corresponded with the limits of built-up urban development at that
time, and in 1965 this area contained about 8 million inhabitants,
including 3 million in the old county, which now became known as
'inner London'.

Because the population was too large for a wholly unified
adminstration, the whole county was divided into 32 boroughs
with about 250,000 people each. Planning and other services best
performed on a large scale were given to the county, and other
functions to the boroughs. A special arrangement was made for
education, with an Inner London Education Authority formed to
cover the area of twelve new boroughs of the old county, but each
of the twenty other boroughs has its own education authority.

The new county of Greater London includes parts of the old
counties of Kent, Surrey, Hertfordshire and Essex and the whole of
the old county of Middlesex, which has ceased to exist as an
administrative area, though the name Middlesex continued to be
used for postal addresses at least up to 1985, and some people who
live in it may still describe it as Middlesex.

Through all this change in the London area, the ancient City of
London has survived as a separate unit of local government and
administration. Greater London covers 600 square miles of land; the
City, its centre and its origin, covers one square mile. The City is
now synonymous with commerce, banking and finance. In 1981 it

63

had 5,000 inhabitants and hardly any hotels. By day its narrow
streets and office blocks, some a hundred years old, some new, are
filled with half a million people. By night and at weekends the area
is deserted, except for the weekend crowds visiting St Paul's
Cathedral, the Tower and some other tourist sites. But this small
area keeps its own Corporation. The Lord Mayor of London (new
each year, like other mayors) is the chief officer of this small area
only, presiding over the needs of its businesses and ceremonies.

After the reforms of 1965, the most important and powerful
person in the government of Greater London was the leader of the
majority party in the Greater London Council. At its 1981 election,
when the Thatcher Conservative government was very unpopular,
Labour won a majority of seats. The Labour group then chose as
leader a man regarded as a left winger. Under his leadership the
council spent large sums of money on social subsidies of every kind
and for purposes not deemed deserving by a government devoted
to economy. In 1984 the government introduced a bill to abolish
the Greater London Council, and to transfer some of its powers to
the 32 boroughs, others to new special boards or joint authorities.

3   Local Government outside London

After London's reforms the question of reform in other parts of
Britain followed. For England the new system introduced in 1974,
on the basis of the Local Government Act of 1972, simplified the
whole system and made it essentially similar to that for London.

England outside London was divided for local government into
45 counties, nine of them are completely new creations, made up of
areas taken away from old counties. The others were mainly based
on the traditional geographical counties, and in most cases kept the
old county-names, but many boundaries were changed and a few
pairs of sparsely-populated counties have been amalgamated.

Each county was subdivided into districts. County councils were
responsible for the big-scale services, especially strategic planning;
district councils for the services run on a smaller scale, such as
housing.

All the counties were given a similar two-tier structure, but the
metropolitan counties' which were formed for the six main
midland and northern industrial conurbations had régimes under
which the second-tier authorities had more powers and functions
than in the 39 other counties.

Some of the new districts are identical with former county boroughs; some are former boroughs with surrounding areas added; some cover bigger areas but include one or more medium-sized towns which may previously have been borough or urban districts. These towns have now only parish councils, with more powers than the old parishes. Parishes now resemble French Communes, but have few functions and powers.

In cases where the population of a new district consists wholly or mainly of people living in the area of a town which was an old borough or city, the district has the name of that town, and it may be given 'borough' or 'city' status. In this case the chairman of the district council has the same title, Mayor or Lord Mayor, as his former equivalent under the old régime. The procedure for deciding whether or not a new district should have borough or city status was typically English. It was left to each new district council (elected in 1973) to decide whether or not it wished to ask the central government to give it this status, the assumption being that the central government would agree, after ensuring that there was no serious local objection.

The industrial conurbations had special needs, partly but not wholly analogous to London's. Industrial development in the nineteenth century produced four major inland towns, Manchester, Sheffield, Leeds and Birmingham, and two major ports, Liverpool on the Mersey and Newcastle on the Tyne. Each of these six principal cities was closely surrounded by several satellite towns which became important in their own right, and in the past fifty years much or most of the intervening land has been filled up by industry and housing. The unpleasant word 'conurbation' first came into use to describe these areas.

The Local Government Act of 1972 created six metropolitan counties, which came into existence in 1974. Four of them, with one to $2\frac{1}{2}$ million people each, and a total near 7 million, formed a continuous belt in the industrial region of the geographical counties of Lancashire and Yorkshire, including the northern part of Cheshire. Further north, Tyneside had nearly a million; West Midlands had 3 million.

All six were completely new, and they had a pattern rather like London. Their 36 districts had between 150,000 and a million inhabitants each, and the district councils were responsible for most of the local services, including education. Within the new county of Greater Manchester, the City of Manchester, with 500,000 people, became one of ten boroughs, but the nine other new boroughs were based on existing satellite towns together with big urban areas around them. Typical is Salford (230,000 people in 1921, 130,000 in 1971) which doubled its population by absorbing a surrounding area of suburbs which now have more people than the old city.

In 1984 the Conservatives introduced legislation for the abolition of the metropolitan counties, so that each borough would have all the normal powers of a county, but with joint boards of the boroughs administering the services common to the region.

4   Ordinary Counties

The other 38 counties have populations between 200,000 and $1\frac{1}{4}$ million each. Most of these counties have about six districts each, and the old county boroughs within them are now districts of the counties. The biggest such district is the City of Bristol (400,000 people), now a district in a new county called Avon, which includes the City of Bath and takes away from Somerset and Gloucestershire all the land within about 30 or 40 kilometres of the centre of Bristol. Wales has eight counties and 37 districts.

The process of making all these changes has been difficult, expensive and painful. Many local government office buildings, including some new ones, are now bigger than they need to be because they are providing fewer services for fewer people than before. Other new functions have to be organised from buildings which are too small for their new purposes. As there are fewer authorities than before, many professional chiefs have either to retire or to accept subordinate positions.

Perhaps the most serious weakness of the changes is that they have greatly reduced the total number of elected councillors. Elections for the new councils were held in the spring of 1973, so that their members could spend a year preparing themselves to take over their new functions. Most of the people elected to be new councillors were already members of the councils which were to be abolished under the new law. With far fewer elected people to control local government, it seems likely that more decisions will need to be left to the permanent officials. However, as councillors have always taken their decisions in committees, which cannot meet very frequently, the new arrangement may lead to less waste of time and less delay. Councillors are now supposed to concentrate on policy, leaving details to the officials.

Although there are now fewer elected councillors in the system as a whole, so that it is more difficult for citizens to tell councillors about their grievances, there is a new ombudsman system. Citizens' grievances can be investigated by these new professional staffs, who will spend all their time on this work, and it is hoped that they will be more effective in protecting citizens against bad administrative practices than the councillors were when they had to do it all themselves.

5 The Working of Local Government

Every county, district and parish has its council, elected by the inhabitants. Any person who is entitled to vote in parliamentary elections may now vote in local elections too. The number of members of a council depends on the population of the area, but is not related to it according to any definite formula. Most of the new county councils have between 40 and 100 members, district councils 30 to 50, parish councils 5 to 20.

The arrangements for the election of the councillors are rather complicated, and are not the same for all types of councils. Members of county councils are elected for three years at general elections taking place every three years. With district councils there may be an election every year, but only one-third of the seats in each council are filled at each annual election; each councillor is elected for three years, but at any particular election only one-third of the seats are filled. Public interest in local government elections is usually rather slight, with 30 to 60% of the people voting. Councillors are not paid for their work, but they may receive an attendance allowance and expenses on a very generous scale in counties and districts.

Every local council has its presiding officer, and this post is filled by the vote of the whole council, for only one year at a time. The presiding officer of a county or district council is called the Chairman, but in a district which is a borough or city he is called Mayor or Lord Mayor. (The title of Lord Mayor is a special mark of distinction given to the mayors of the seventeen most important English cities, and of Cardiff in Wales. A Lord Mayor does not receive any title personally by virtue of his office.)

The mayor has many formal duties, as the first citizen of his town. He has a chain of office, which he wears on official occasions.

In modern times it has been thought that the mayor needs to have a female consort on social and formal occasions, and in most towns the mayor appoints a woman to be his mayoress. If the mayor is married he normally appoints his wife; indeed she may even have pushed him to seek office in the first place for the sake of the social benefits which she will eventually derive from being mayoress. These days it is quite usual for the office of mayor or lord mayor to be held by a woman, as many women are elected in their own right to local councils. In that case there is still a mayoress in addition to the mayor, and the mayoress must be a woman. Thus if the mayor is a woman or an unmarried man, it is usual for some suitable female relative of the mayor to be made mayoress; it has been known for a niece of fifteen years old to have this job. If there are no suitable female relatives, then a friend must be chosen.

What types of people are elected to local councils? It is not easy to generalise. Many councillors are shopkeepers, businessmen or housewives, and many are industrial workers. The motives for trying to be elected are a mixture of a spirit of public service and a desire for power and prestige. A man may derive some indirect advantages for his business through being a member of a local council, just because he makes many contacts and becomes more widely known in the community; but there is very little complaint of any attempts to obtain direct financial advantages through any sort of corruption. The standards of honesty maintained in all sections of public life are usually high, but recently some huge networks of bribery have been uncovered.

Since the rise of the Labour Party local politics have become more and more dominated by the parties. The Labour members of a council are nearly always subject to a strict party discipline, and whenever an important decision is to come before a council it is usual for the Labour members to have a preliminary private meeting at which they decide how they will vote. Once that decision has been made, the Labour Party expects its councillors to vote as the party has decided, and there have been many cases of Labour councillors being expelled from the group for disobedience. Some councils have Labour majorities, and with these it seems that the real decisions are made on behalf of the council by the preliminary meeting of Labour councillors.

By now, two-party government is a usual characteristic of important local councils, with the Labour Party opposed by Conservatives, though there may also be some Liberals or

Independents. The strength of party discipline among non-Labour members varies from place to place, and it depends on the way the parties are balanced. If Labour is strong, then the other side also tends to be strongly disciplined and to vote together, but if there are very few Labour members the non-Labour people may be really independent in their voting.

Before the 1972 reforms the elections to many of the smaller councils, particularly in rural districts, were kept free of party. The amalgamation into bigger units increased the domination of the major parties. In the elections of 1975–7 all but two of the English county councils, and four-fifths of the district councils, were composed mainly on a party basis. The reforms had failed significantly to increase the proportion of the people bothering to vote. Most of those who voted, voted Labour or Conservative mainly because of their preference in terms of national politics. Although Labour was in power in the central government all through this period, the Labour Party's current unpopularity was reflected in the results of local elections. After the elections of the spring of 1977 the Conservatives controlled 40 of the 45 English counties, Labour 3. The next county council elections, in 1981, took place after two years of Conservative central control, and the unpopularity of Mrs Thatcher's government at that time gave Labour control in all six metropolitan counties and twelve others.

All local councils work through committees. Each council has a committee for each of the main sections of its work; the general management of the schools in a county or a metropolitan district is under the control of the education committee of the county or district council. Some of the committees consist only of members of the council (with the parties represented in the same proportion as in the whole council), and some of them have in addition a few co-opted members—people who do not belong to the council but have been chosen by the whole council to assist the committee with their special knowledge or other qualifications. For very important matters the committee can only recommend to the council what is to be done, and the decision is made by the council in general session. Meetings are normally open to the public.

The local authorities appoint their own staffs. At the middle and higher levels of the local government service the local government officers are usually ready to move from one place to another, and it is often necessary to move in order to get promotion. The appointment of the local councils' staffs is supposed to have nothing to do with politics, though inevitably politics may have something to do with some of the top appointments. If the political majority of a council changes as a result of an election, it is not to be expected that there will be changes among the professional staff as a result. The 1974 reforms caused a great upheaval.

Discussion of the finance of local government involves a broader discussion of the whole of its purpose. To begin with, we may say that each local council performs services which are of value to the local inhabitants who benefit from the services. This principle suggests that the local inhabitants ought to pay for the services, and to be free to decide, through their elected councillors, how much they want to pay. But the modern local government system is almost entirely the result of decisions by the national Parliament, and most of the tasks which local councils perform are tasks which the central authorities have told them they must perform. The nation is interested in the way in which the local councils do their work, and the central government exercises some supervision and gives some financial assistance.

Local authorities are allowed to impose taxes on their residents in only one form—a tax collected from all people who occupy land or buildings, based on an objective assessment of the value. These local taxes are called 'rates'. Every house, shop, etc., has a 'rateable value'. assessed by officials of the central government. The local tax is imposed by each local authority as a percentage of the rateable value.

The rates for county and district purposes are collected by officers of the districts, and the district must hand over to the county the proportion due to it. Some areas are more prosperous than others. In the district of the Borough of Guildford the rateable value of all property was in 1977 assessed at £185 per inhabitant, in the Metropolitan Borough of Barnsley at £80. Guildford is in the county of Surrey, the whole of which has a rateable value per person twice as great as the county of South Yorkshire, which includes Barnsley. Yet in Barnsley and its county the demands on the local authority are likely to be greater than those in Guildford and the county of Surrey.

In order to cope with this problem the central government makes grants to the counties and districts, calculated according to complicated formulae; and some of the particular expenditures of local authorities are almost entirely paid from central funds.

Rather more than half of the total revenue of local authorities comes from the central grants, paid out of general tax revenue. After 1975 the Labour government began to restrict its grants, and their Conservative successors were even more restrictive. Faced with reduced central grants, some local councils increased their rate demands beyond a level which the central government considered reasonable. The Conservative manifesto of 1983 promised legislation 'to curb excessive and irresponsible rate increases by high-spending councils', and in 1984 the government introduced a bill to put this plan into effect. It was attacked as a completely new central interference with such local autonomy as local councils still enjoyed, and caused serious divisions within the Conservative Party itself. But so long as voting in local elections is largely determined by the voters' current preferences among the national parties, increasing central interference seems inevitable.

Local authority manpower: by service, 1979 and 1983		
Great Britain	thousands	
	1979	1983
Education - lecturers and teachers	638.5	611.5
- others	472.9	428.1
Construction	155.9	137.2
Transport	31.4	28.1
Social services	233.0	245.5
Public libraries and museums	36.6	36.5
Recreation, parks, and baths	84.9	86.4
Environmental health	23.9	23.2
Refuse collection and disposal	60.3	53.0
Housing	53.5	59.0
Town and country planning	23.5	22.7
Fire service - regular	39.0	40.1
- others	5.9	5.7
Miscellaneous services	300.0	286.2
Police - all ranks	123.0	134.1
- cadets	3.9	1.4
- civilians	38.4	40.6
- traffic wardens	5.2	5.3
Agency staff	0.5	0.6
Magistrates' courts/district courts	8.1	9.1
Probation - officers	5.0	5.8
- others	4.2	5.4
Total	2347.7	2265.7

Question
Discuss the changes in numbers in 1979–83.

The Central Law Courts in London.

5

Law, the Courts and the Police

England and Wales have a single system of law and courts, and
Scotland has a system of its own; this chapter will deal only with
England and Wales. The first thing to notice is that there is no civil
code and no criminal code. The law as a whole consists partly of
statutes, or Acts of Parliament, and partly of common law which
may be said to be made up of past decisions of judges, with regard
to matters not regulated by statutes, in accordance with custom and
reason and the previous decisions of courts. A large part of the civil
law is not contained in statutes at all but made up of a mass of
precedents, previous court decisions, interpreted in authoritative
legal text books. By now, however, almost all actions for which a
person may be punished are actions which are specifically forbidden
by some statute or other, with the statute usually including a
provision for a maximum penalty. It is almost as though there were
a sort of criminal code scattered through a large number of laws.

The legal system has generally been respected for its fairness, but
criticised for its cumbersome arrangements and for the techniques
of mystification by which those who operate it ensure their own
indispensability and their privileges. The division between solicitors
and barristers is said to increase the cost of litigation to the
advantage of the lawyers. Solicitors work mainly in their offices,
barristers in the courts. Barristers provide the reservoir from which
the higher judges are drawn, and their profession is so organised
that it is difficult to achieve success without some initial financial
security. Most higher barristers, if not the sons of lawyers, are
themselves the sons of members of the professional and managerial
classes, and have been educated in the privileged private sector.
Some Leftist commentators claim that the courts share and protect
the values of established privileged groups.

The barristers' sense of caste is reinforced by a genuine tradition of independence of the executive government: not merely independence but even a certain healthy rivalry with it. The courts and the people who work them are not the servants of the executive. Judges are appointed by the Crown, but on the advice of people of the law and on grounds of legal competence. Once appointed they cannot easily be removed. Their independence is not new; Montesquieu was deeply impressed by it in the eighteenth century. They may and do check the executive government, for apparent invasions of private rights not clearly sanctioned by the laws passed by Parliament.

The role of the ordinary courts, and of the barristers and judges who work in them, has been enhanced in the twentieth century by the growth of a new kind of special litigation arising from newly-created rights of citizens against the state. England has no supreme administrative court, but there are countless special tribunals to adjudicate disputed claims for industrial injury compensation, or for national insurance benefits, etc. Special tribunals have been created for the settlement of such disputes, usually presided over by barristers; and in some cases a final appeal may be made to the ordinary couts.

Barristers and judges lack one final power. There is no written constitution, hence no constitutional court. Parliament is sovereign. So the courts cannot question the authority of the constitutional validity of the statutes; they can only interpet them. But the process of interpretation may give them a role which borders the political.

1   The Courts and their Judicial Officers

There are two main kinds of courts, and two kinds of judicial officers to correspond with them. Courts of first instance are worked by magistrates, who are normally Justices of the Peace; higher courts ('Crown' courts) by judges, or in some cases, senior barristers specially appointed to perform judicial functions for part of their time.

Magistrates' courts

Every person charged with an offence is summoned to appear before a local magistrates' court, which may impose a fine up to a general limit of £2,000 or twelve months' imprisonment, though for some specified offences the laws prescribe maximum penalties below these limits. With 98% of cases the magistrates on the bench decide on guilt or innocence, and if necessary what penalty to impose. With more serious cases the magistrates can decide only to send them for trial in a crown court, where the decision on guilt or innocence will be made by a jury of twelve citizens chosen by chance, and if necessary the penalty decided by the presiding judge, helped by two Justices of the Peace (J.P.s). A person accused before a magistrates' court may demand to be sent for trial before a crown court, even if the case is one with which in general the magistrates could have dealt themselves.

A magistrates' court normally consits of three J.P.s (occasionally, two or four or more). The J.P.s are ordinary but worthy citizens who have been appointed to their positions by the Lord Chancellor on the advice of local appointing committees. J.P.s have no formal qualifications; they are chosen merely for their good reputation, often with the support of political parties or approved voluntary bodies. Once appointed, they are expected to attend a few weekend courses of instruction about their work, and to read material sent to them at intervals. There are 25,000 J.P.s in England; each of them works in the courts on about 30 to 50 days a year. Those who have jobs must take time off, and receive a small compensation for loss of earnings; but otherwise the J.P.s receive no payment for their work. Attempts are now being made to ensure that J.P.s are of widely differing social backgrounds, but inevitably most are middle class. About one-third of them are women—mostly housewives who do not have paid jobs.

In their courts the J.P.s are advised on points of law by their Clerks, who are professional lawyers; otherwise they decide each case brought before them according to their sense of what is fair and suitable, within the limits of their powers, and with some attention to general guidance which they receive. There are a few special exceptions to the general pattern. Some of the courts in London and in ten other towns have stipendiary magistrates, who are qualified lawyers, work full time and are paid salaries; but there are only fifty stipendiary magistrates in England, and a few in Wales.

Crown courts

When a criminal case is not dealt with finally in a magistrates' court it goes for trial in a crown court. The court is presided over by a judge, but the decision on guilt or innocence is made by a jury of twelve citizens chosen by lot from the list of persons entitled to vote in elections. The judge's functions are, first, to see that the trial is properly conducted, second, to give guidance to the jury before asking it for its verdict, and finally, if the jury finds the accused 'guilty', to decide upon the penalty and 'pronounce sentence'. For this last decision the judge is helped by two J.P.s who have been sitting beside him throughout the proceedings.

About a hundred towns have crown courts, but only a quarter of these are 'first-tier' courts, at which the most important civil and criminal cases are heard before high court judges. Other cases may be heard before circuit judges, whose full-time appointments are mostly attached to one or other of the six regional 'circuits'. Appeals are heard in London before three appeal judges.

Judges are either practising or former barristers. The judge in a crown court may be one of several types of people, but all share two things in common. First, they are all qualified, professional and experienced lawyers, chosen for their competence in the law but with no formal sociological qualifications to help them with the business of sentencing prisoners, and second, they are paid for their work.

There are not enough high court and circuit judges to supply the needs of the crown courts without intolerable delay. (The English system has been more insistent than some others on reasonable speed in bringing cases up for trial.) The gap is filled by senior barristers who spend most of their time arguing civil or criminal cases, representing either defendants or civil plaintiffs or the prosecuting side in criminal cases, but who spend some days or weeks each year presiding over courts. About 400 barristers hold titular office as 'Recorders'; others are appointed *ad hoc* as deputy judges, and paid fees for each day of work. Barristers who are appointed to permanent positions as high court judges have often been recorders.

In a crown court a person who is accused of a crime, when he is brought into the 'dock', is asked by the Clerk if he is guilty or not guilty. If he says that he is not guilty, he must be tried in order to establish whether he is in fact guilty or not. For this purpose a jury has to be appointed. There will be sitting in a special section of the court about thirty local citizens (male or female) who have had their names chosen by lot from the electoral register, and who have been ordered to attend at the court to be ready to serve as members of juries. From this group of citizens twelve will be called out to be the jury for the particular case; both the prosecution and the defence may object to any person who is called out for the jury (for example, because the person happens to be personally acquainted with someone who is concerned in the case), and if that happens one of the other waiting jurors is put in his place. Either side may object to up to seven jurors without giving reasons.

When the jury is in its place for the trial (the 'jury box' is a small enclosure, usually at the side of the court) the trial begins. The prosecution builds up its case by presenting witnesses, who are questioned by the prosecuting barrister (or 'counsel'), so that a story of the supposed crime is built up. Each witness may be cross-examined by the other side on the evidence which he has given. When the prosecution has finished presenting its case, the defence may call witnesses, including the accused person himself, in an attempt to show that he is innocent; these witnesses may also be cross-examined by the other side. The rules of evidence are important and complicated; in particular, evidence of which a witness does not have direct knowledge is not normally allowed.

When this is all finished, the judge summarises the evidence for the benefit of the jury, tells them of any points of law involved, and presents to them the problem which they have to decide. Then the twelve members of the jury are taken to a room where they are locked in and left alone until they agree on a verdict. If after some hours they return to the court and say that they cannot agree, a new trial must be held. A person accused cannot be found to be guilty except by the verdict of at least ten of the twelve members of the jury. Normally the jury do agree, though sometimes only after some hours of discussion. Most of them have probably never had any experience of this kind of activity before, and a few strong personalities may have much influence on the others.

If the jury finds the accused guilty, then it is for the judge to 'pronounce sentence'. If the accused has pleaded guilty in the first place, then no trial has been necessary, and the court has been able to go straight to the business of deciding on his punishment. Before the judge pronounces sentence, a police witness gives evidence about any previous convictions of the prisoner, and also about his character as far as the police know anything about it. The prisoner may speak too, and others may speak on his behalf. A person may appeal to the Court of Criminal Appeal againt conviction or sentence, and the appeal court may quash the conviction (for example, on the ground that the judge did not direct the jury properly), or it may reduce or increase the sentence. The highest court of all is the House of Lords: ten Lords of Appeal in Ordinary. Any five of these form the 'House of Lords' in its capacity as the final court of appeal—though the Lord Chancellor and Lord Chief Justice (who is primarily president of the Queen's Bench Division) may be among the five for any particular case.

2   Crime and Punishment

If a person is found guilty of a fairly small offence, and has no previous convictions, he may receive no punishment at all, but be told that if he does wrong again the first offence will be taken into account along with the next. Or he may be placed on probation for a period—left at liberty, but under the supervision of a probation officer, who is a trained, professional social worker. Punishments are in the form of fines or imprisonment, and some offenders are given suspended prison sentences—a recent innovation. The death penalty for murder was first abolished for a five-year period in 1965. It was then completely abolished in 1969, although opinion polls seemed to show that over two-thirds of the public were in favour of it.

Meanwhile some other types of crime, including crimes of violence and theft, have increased very disturbingly in recent years, and many crimes are committed by young people. The prisons are overcrowded, with many cells intended for one man occupied by three. At the same time, there seems to be some confusion about the purpose of punishment. The fear of punishment, and in particular of prison, is intended to deter people from committing crimes, but when they have committed their crimes they are not likely to be reformed by life in prison, where they often have to live in drab and dreary conditions, with too little to occupy them.

All the prisons are under the control of the Home Secretary through the Prison Board. Several reforms have been carried through in recent years. Some attempt is made to classify prisoners and give appropriate treatment to each one. There are opportunities for prisoners to learn trades and to attend classes on many subjects, and prison régimes are not intended to be repressive. Unfortunately, it seems that many aspects of prison life which cause positive discomfort or humiliation to the prisoners are not devised as instruments of punishment, but arise from the physical nature of the prison buildings—most of which are around a hundred years old. Thus prisoners feel that the indignities that they suffer are

Pentonville prison, one of the oldest prisons in London.

wrongly imposed upon them, and they are led to feel cynical about the attempts to help them in a positive way, which for administrative reasons are often not carried out with any real or convincing determination.

Many of the people in prison are still waiting to be tried in a crown court, having been remanded in custody by magistrates week after week. People who are sentenced to imprisonment are released after serving two-thirds of their sentences, and increasing numbers are being released earlier 'on parole'.

Young offenders may be placed in the care of the local authority, whose Social Services officers decide exactly what to do; usually they send young people to special schools. A new device, used for young people aged from 10 to 21 years, is the order to go to an 'attendance centre' on a specified number of Saturdays. Also an offender may be sentenced to a maximum of 240 hours of 'community service' as an alternative to prison. This new device was first used experimentally in Nottingham in 1973, and has now come into general use in places where the necessary provision has been made available. It can only be used if the offender agrees to co-operate.

3   The Legal Profession

The legal profession consists of two elements, barristers and
solicitors, and the two elements must be clearly distinguished.
Solicitors, who are sometimes called the junior branch, are much
the more numerous. When a person needs the assistance of the law,
either because he has a dispute, or because he is in trouble, or
because he is buying or selling a house or other property, or
concerned with a question of inheritance of property, he must go to
a solicitor. The average problem, particularly a straightforward
transfer of property, can be dealt with finally by solicitors, who can
also speak for their clients in magistrates' courts. If a case, civil or
criminal, is more serious or difficult, or has to be heard in a higher
court, a client's solicitor engages a barrister to whom he hands over
the task of representing the client in the court.

In order to become a solicitor a person must spend some time
working in the office of an already established firm of solicitors, and
successfully pass the examinations of the Law Society. Solicitors
usually work together in partnerships, or 'firms', being helped by
clerks and having the usual array of any office.

To be a barrister a man must be a member of one of the four
Inns of Court and pass the Bar examination. He must also keep
twelve terms as a student at his Inn; to do this he must attend on six
evenings during each term for the purpose of eating dinner in the
Hall. He may do this while he is earning his living, provided that
he is not earning it by working as a solicitor or solicitor's clerk, or
he may do it while he is a student at a university. When a young
barrister begins his professional career he must join the 'chambers'
of an established barrister, and for some years is usually able to earn
very little money. If he is efficient and enjoys good luck, however,
he can do very well once he becomes well established in the
profession. Eventually he may have an opportunity of being
appointed a Queen's Counsel; if he does 'take silk' (as this process is
called), he may then only appear in court as a leader, assisted by
another established barrister. Very big incomes and great
reputations can be won by a Queen's Counsel but a really succesful
barrister must live a life of exceptionally hard work. The House of
Commons includes about ninety barristers among its members. If
they are appointed as judges they must give up their seats in the
House of Commons

There is no judicial profession in England; high court judges,
circuit judges and full-time paid magistrates or stipendiaries are

appointed from among barristers of long standing. If a barrister accepts a job as a stipendiary magistrate or as a circuit judge he is unlikely to be promoted to a higher judicial post.

Although judges are well paid their current earnings are less than those which successful barristers can make. An established barrister may accept appointment as a full-time judge, even at some sacrifice of current income, for any of a combination of reasons: higher status, easier life, and the prospect of a pension when he retires. The basic grade is that of a circuit judge. There are about 300 circuit judges, each working mainly in one area of the country.

At a higher level are nearly 50 high court judges, of the Queen's Bench Division, paid 50% more than circuit judges. They have the title 'Mr Justice Smith', etc., and are all based in London, but spend some of their time visiting the more important provincial crown courts to hear the most important and most difficult cases. There are also about 30 other judges in the Chancery and Family Divisions of the High Court of Justice, who deal only with civil cases, almost all in London.

The High Court of Justice has several Divisions. The Chancery Division consists of the Lord Chancellor and ten judges, and deals with questions of company law, bankruptcy, trusts, the administration of the estates of people who have died, and some other matters of the same general type. The Probate, Divorce and Admiralty Division has been replaced by a new Family Division, which deals with divorce and questions arising out of wills. All the judges of these two Divisions remain in London. The Queen's Bench Division consists of the Lord Chief Justice and about fifty other judges. These divide their time between civil work in London, the Central Criminal Court (or 'Old Bailey'), also in London, and visits to the provincial crown courts. The old ceremonial which used to be associated with the assize courts was abolished with the reform of 1972, though the high court judges still wear robes and big wigs in court, and other judges and barristers wear very formal clothes, and small light grey wigs, which are rather uncomfortable in hot weather.

The reforms of 1972 have not made litigation any cheaper. The high earnings of barristers are paid for by the people who are unwise enough or unfortunate enough to need to employ them, but there is a system of legal aid through which poorer people's legal costs are paid.

The English legal system enjoys a good reputation for fairness. A person accused of an offence is sure of a fair and open trial, and enjoys good protection against the possibility of an unfair decision. Justice, both civil and criminal, operates with reasonable speed and the excellent system of free legal aid and advice to people with low incomes is of great benefit. The magistrates' courts are often criticised on the ground that the Justices of the Peace are not professionally trained, but their critics may forget that the most important part of their work, that of imposing penalties on minor wrongdoers, is essentially social rather than legal in character. At the same time there is very much less complaint about the lack of social or criminological training of some of the High Court Judges, who have to pass sentence in the more serious cases.

4　The Police

One of the most English institutions is the English policeman, with his odd helmet reminiscent of the topees that sahibs used to wear in India. To an Englishman a motorised policeman with a flat-topped cap looks somehow a little less reassuring, more likely to be an enemy, than one with a helmet. Outside London the police are all local forces, employed and paid by county councils. Separate town police forces were abolished by the reform of local government in 1974. The central government gives the local authorities grants towards the cost of policing. Inspectors from the Home Office visit the local forces, and the Home Secretary can approve or disapprove of appointments and removals of Chief Constables, but the actions of a local police force are normally not the responsibility of any minister. In London the régime is different. The Metropolitan Police, whose zone of operation covers Greater London, is under the direct responsibility of the Home Secretary, as good order in the capital concerns the central government. The Metropolitan Police provides certain national police services, including the maintenance of a national registry of all criminals and crimes, to which local police forces may refer. The famous 'Scotland Yard' is the Criminal Investigation Department, which gets its popular name from New Scotland Yard, where its officers are situated, close to Whitehall and the Houses of Parliament.

During the twentieth century the English police forces have become well-known throughout the world from the great mass of fiction about crime and detection poured out by so many English authors and often translated into many other languages. Any regular reader of English detective stories is familiar with the name of Scotland Yard and its detectives, and also with the figure of the ordinary English policeman, whether he be a member of the Metropolitan Police Force or a member of one of the local forces. The modern policeman needs a great variety of new professional skills to enable him to deal with new-style crime and with the other problems which afflict life in Britain no less than other countries. Moving mostly in cars rather than on foot, the police are less obviously in contact with the public than in the past. When going about their normal work the police do not carry guns: they themselves prefer to be unarmed. The recent increase of criminal violence has left Britain less violent than many similar countries, and there is a special public revulsion against people who use violence against the police. One recent change has come through the adoption of a new system for dealing with complaints against the police, devised to ensure that the complaints are properly investigated. Over 20,000 complaints were lodged in 1977, and 100 policemen punished.

Policemen dealing with a group of pickets.

Meanwhile, the police in their turn have given expression to their own discontents. They have joined in the widespread pressure for higher pay, and demanded to be exempted from the limits imposed by Government policies against inflation. At a big assembly of policemen in 1977 the Home Secretary was confronted by loud and angry shouting. Sir Robert Mark, who was head of the Metropolitan Police from 1971 to 1976, spoke publicly of the difficulties and discouragements with which the police had to contend. He noted that in some criminal trials barristers defending guilty people were too much inclined to try to secure acquittal on technical grounds, by exploiting the protection given by legal rules to accused people. It is not pleasant for a policeman to spend a Saturday dealing with violent mobs of football supporters or political demonstrators—particularly when he may be injured or unjustly accused of being violent himself. Meanwhile, opinion polls showed that the majority of the public sympathised with the police and thought their conditions of work should be improved.

A policeman engaged in more pleasant duties at a London street carnival.

Notifiable offences recorded by the police in England and Wales			
	thousands		
	1971	1981	1982
Notifiable offences recorded			
Violence against the person	47.0	100.2	108.7
Sexual offences	23.6	19.4	19.7
Burglary	451.5	723.2	810.6
Robbery	7.5	20.3	22.8
Theft and handling stolen goods	1003.7	1603.2	1755.9
Fraud and forgery	99.8	106.7	123.1
Criminal damage	27.0	—	174.1
Other offences	5.6	4.1	3.8
Total notifiable offences	1665.7	2577.1	3018.7

Questions

1. Explain the difference, in England, between a magistrate and a judge.
2. When lawyers earn large sums of money, why do people want to work as magistrates for nothing?

Above: The London Stock Exchange.
Below: Tilbury dockworkers voting at a trade union meeting.

6

Work and Money

1   The Structure of Trade and Industry

Many people say that the British do not work hard enough, and
there may be some truth in this complaint. Certainly for some years
past, production in Britain has been increasing much more slowly
than in most European countries, and the lack of progress is causing
great concern. Some blame the managements, too secure in the
enjoyment of their privileges and expense accounts and too well
protected by their trade associations. Others blame the workers,
over-anxious to protect their jobs and to resist labour-saving
techniques. Some say that there is not enough incentive, that if a
man is successful he only pays more taxes, that if he is lazy the
unions and the welfare state protect him. Others blame the
economic policy of the Government for not doing enough to
encourage investment in the 'right' directions. All these arguments
have some justification.

    The standard working week is generally forty hours, though
very many workers work a few extra hours at overtime rates. For
factory workers, except those on shift-work, the working week is
often spread over five days, Monday to Friday, with each day
beginning at about 8 a.m. and interrupted by one or two tea-breaks
and a longer interval for lunch in the middle of the day. Offices and
shops are usually open from 9 a.m. to 5 or 5.30. Since 1970 banks
and most offices have stayed shut on Saturdays. Shops have a five-
and-a-half-day week, closing for the afternoon on the local 'early
closing day', which is Wednesday or Thursday in most towns.
Except in small towns few people can go home in the middle of the
day, as they have long distances to travel from home to workplace;
in London the journey is for many people an hour or more each
way. Many large organisations provide canteens where their staffs
can get lunch quickly and cheaply; other people mostly provide

themselves with sandwiches or have snacks in pubs, or choose between the many types of small restaurants that have grown up in the past few years.

The process whereby people find jobs, and employers find workers, is helped by the job centres run by the Government. But advertisements in newspapers are very much used too, particularly for specialist jobs. Fortunately for the newspapers, advertisers do not use abbreviations as much as in France and their notices are a useful source of general information.

The British economic system, while nominally capitalist, is now really a complex combination of several systems, and pure capitalism is probably a smaller element than in any other West European country. People's perceptions of the system are determined more by prejudices and myths than by facts; and terms like 'free enterprise', 'competition', 'the workers', 'the capitalist class', 'monopoly capitalism' and 'exploitation' are used with varying and uncertain meaning, often so as to express prejudice rather than any objective reality.

About one-third of all goods and services are produced by central or local government or by state-owned corporations. A third of all people who contribute to the economy by their work are employed by publicly-owned bodies. Most energy production is socialised: production and distribution of electricity and gas, production (but not distribution) of coal, part of the production and distribution of oil (B.P. is part-owned by the Government); the iron and steel producing industry (1949–51 and again since 1966). The state owns the railways, most buses, some lorries, most public transport aeroplanes, nearly all important airports, water supply, radio, two out of four television channels, posts and telephones. Local authorities, with state support, are responsible for roads, for the welfare services and for 90% of education. Nearly all treatment of sickness is run by the National Health Service.

The other two-thirds of the economy is within the private sector, shared unequally between public companies, private companies and individuals. Much the greater part of this is owned and controlled by public companies. At least one-tenth of the economy is owned by foreign companies, mostly American, and some by multi-national companies, many of which are partly British.

More than half of the private sector is owned by large companies with typically the following characteristics: at least two-thirds of the capital is owned by institutions—insurance companies and pension funds, using money contributed by more than half of the population to funds to supplement their retirement benefits from the national insurance scheme; banks, public bodies of all sorts, including local councils, investing the public's money; trade unions; and other companies. The other one-third is owned by individual shareholders—several tens of thousands of them, no single one of whom owns as much as a one-thousandth part of the whole capital. A large part of the privately-owned capital is owned by retired people, particularly widows, many of them poor. There is a Monopolies Commission whose task is to ensure that competition is not removed by price-fixing agreements or by the process of amalgamation, by which big companies are constantly absorbing their rivals in pursuit of greater efficiency in production.

A company's Board of ten to twenty directors contains men co-opted for skills and experience, as assessed by the existing members, in technical or financial aspects of the company's affairs. Some work part-time, most full-time for the company with executive responsibilites. Some have been promoted to the Board from the employed staff, others brought in from outside. Some began their careers as manual workers, others began as qualified specialists or graduate general management trainees. Almost no firms include any women at all among their directors.

Companies are obliged to publish the numbers of directors and employees earning over £30,000 a year, with details but not names. Most full-time directors of large companies are paid salaries between £30,000 and £90,000 a year, giving them a 'take-home' salary after tax amounting to about six or seven times the average employee's take-home pay. Directors are usually shareholders, but in most large companies they own together less than one-thousandth part of the whole ordinary capital, and their income from dividends, after tax, is insignificant. A few company-boards include one or two descendants of the man who built up the business in an earlier generation, and these may have significant shareholdings, often in a family trust.

The controllers of large-scale industry and commerce are rewarded by salaries and fringe benefits. Any notion that they personally enjoy the profits is, for the most part, pure mythology. The two main exceptions are in small or new and rising firms, which together form only a small part of the private sector as a whole. The shape of capitalism has been largely transformed by the managerial revolution.

In 1977 the report of a committee on industrial democracy (Chairman, Lord Bullock) proposed that half of the directors of large companies should be appointed by the trade unions of their employees. The Labour Party's programme for the future includes an intention to implement this plan, which is opposed by those currently engaged in management because they argue that decisions such as those which directors have to take are best taken by people chosen for their competence in technology or management, and who have a common purpose of maximising efficiency—as was still the case in 1978 in both the public and the private sector.

2 Taxes, Incomes and the Standard of Living

Direct taxes on personal income provide the State with its biggest source of revenue. The basic rate of income tax was 30 per cent in 1981–84, as compared with 40 per cent in the 1960s and 45 to 50 per cent in the first post-war years. For the individual the allowances and sliding scales (which change every year) are more important than the basic rate. A person with less than half the average income pays no tax at all; one with an average income pays about 20 per cent of the whole. The higher the income, the bigger the proportion paid in tax. A person with ten times the average keeps just over half: much more than at any time in the past forty years.

Labour governments use income tax deliberately to redistribute from rich to poor; Conservatives think that high taxes discourage effort and ambition. Their tax changes after 1979 had little effect on the average man; but in 1984–5 the tax on unearned income above seven times the average wage was 60 per cent, compared with 98 per cent under Labour in 1978.

Employers are required to deduct tax from weekly pay-packets or monthly cheques, and there is meticulous calculation of incomes, so as to determine the exact liability to tax. Much of the best and most highly-paid talent in the country is employed in calculating the liability to tax of individuals and companies, and the huge staff of the Inland Revenue increased, even during the period of cutbacks in teaching, hospitals and other public services in 1975–7.

The high rates of income tax have to some extent counteracted the effects of the increase in wages and salaries which has for many years exceeded the increase in productivity. Successive governments, Labour and Conservative, have taken action at times of crisis to limit wage increase. In 1971–2 the Conservatives imposed limits by law, and the limits were more severe on higher than on lower earnings. In the 3¼ years of Conservative government (1970–3), with a general upward trend in production, average real disposable incomes of the lowest-paid decile of male manual workers rose by 12% while the highest-paid rose by 10% and the more highly-paid non-manual workers by much less than this. But inflation reached 10%.

In 1974, when Labour came into power, the limits were removed. Labour sought a voluntary agreement with the unions, called the 'social contract'. However, during that year one union after another was successful in obtaining a very big wage rise. Meanwhile, actual production began to fall, so the wage rises led to higher prices. The British consumed more than they produced, and the excess consumption was made possible by loans from foreign countries. Prices rose by almost 30% in a year, and the value of the British currency in relation to others fell. It was clear that the excess of consumption over production could not indefinitely be financed by borrowing money.

In 1975 the Labour Government secured the agreement of the unions to a system of restraint in wage-increases, under which all wages could rise by a uniform fixed amount, but people earning more than three times the average wage received no pay increase at all. Their real net purchasing power was thus drastically reduced by the rise in prices.

The policy ensured that the consequences of the decline in real national product affected the better-off seriously, while the lower-paid people suffered very little. In the years 1974–6 the real disposable earnings of the lowest-paid decile of male manual workers remained static, while the median manual real earnings declined by 3% and those of the top decile declined by 6%. Real incomes of people other than manual workers at the higher levels declined drastically, so that there was a very rapid reduction in inequality. Another important group who suffered a severe loss of living standards were those who became unemployed, particularly people who had previously been relatively well paid. As the number of unemployed rose, so the number who suffered for this reason grew. However, some of those who had previously worked for relatively low wages but became unemployed did not suffer a serious loss of living standards, because the social security payments kept pace with inflation and were about equal to the lowest earnings of people at work.

By 1979 1½ million people were unemployed—about 6 per cent of the available labour force. The rate was much higher in the traditional areas of heavy industry, western Scotland, Wales and parts of northern England. Although inflation had been cut in 1977 to an annual rate of 10 per cent, it was now rising again. When Mrs Thatcher's Conservative government took office one of its aims was to attack inflation. A second was to reduce public expenditure. A third was to find a new way to make British industry more efficient—by leaving it to compete in a harsh economic climate. In the next five years inflation was indeed reduced, from an annual rate of over 15 per cent in 1979–80 to 5 per cent in 1984. Public expenditure did not fall; it rose, even as a proportion of the gross national product. Industry did not quickly become more efficient. Many firms went out of business. Others, to keep alive, reduced their staffs and secured union agreement to more efficient working practices, so that new machines and methods of production could be put to good use. Unemployment rose, reaching 3 million in 1982, then changing very little in the next two years. In Britain as a whole, one person in seven was then out of work; by 1983 one person in fifteen had been six months or more without a job. The difference between the relatively prosperous south of England and the rest of Britain became sharper than ever before, and there was especial concern about the unemployment of young people in the North.

By 1984 there were a few encouraging signs. Industrial production per person employed was rising faster than in Germany; the total volume of production returned to the level of five years before and was rising. The national balance of payments was in surplus but this improvement from the huge deficits of the mid–1970s was largely due to the benefits of North Sea oil. And it was fair to complain that this temporary advantage was not being used for some much needed investment in the public capital stock, from sewers to roads and railways.

Real wage costs have continued to rise faster in Britain than in Germany, particularly with the improvement in the economy in 1982–4. It also seems that the British have for many years spent more of their net incomes on consumption (instead of investment) than most other European people. It has been argued that this is partly because the rewards of investment have for many years been discouraging—though these improved in 1982–4.

For British people who have not suffered from unemployment for long periods, living standards have risen steadily, though less rapidly than in most other European countries. Four-fifths of households now have telephones and refrigerators, two-thirds have cars, two-thirds own their houses. The British were once notorious for their cold houses and unpalatable food, but these deficiencies have been attacked with continuing vigour. Two-thirds of homes now have central heating—twice as many as ten years ago; and the food available in shops and restaurants has improved so much in quality and variety of choice that the old criticisms are no longer valid. But while living standards have risen, expectations have risen faster still, and it is significant that while the average working week has been reduced, to less than forty hours, the average hours of overtime work, paid for at above the normal rate, have consistently remained high by European standards, even in the years of high unemployment.

3   Trade Unions

Apart from some small independent professional associations, all British trade unions (of which there are about a hundred, some big, some small) are affiliated to a single national body, the Trades Union Congress, from which the Labour Party grew. As T.U.C. unions hold four-fifths of the voting weight at the Labour Party Conference, two-fifths in the electoral college which elects the leader of the Labour Party, and (since 1979) most Labour M.P.s are sponsored by unions, their relationship with the Labour Party is close. Total membership of all T.U.C. unions grew from a million in 1900 to six million in 1920. After the unsuccessful general strike of 1926 the membership declined in the 1930s but then rose again, to 12 million, or more than half of all employed people, by 1979. By then white collar unions such as the Association of Scientific, Technical and Managerial Staffs, with over 400,000 members, accounted for a quarter of the total membership. In 1979–84 most unions lost membership—the membership of the biggest (Transport and General Workers) fell from 2 to 1.5 million—and the total of members fell to around ten million.

Most unions are connected with particular trades, but there are curious anomalies. Railway manual workers, including some train-drivers, belong to the National Union of Railwaymen, but most drivers belong to their own union (A.S.L.E.F.); if the A.S.L.E.F.

decides that its drivers are to strike, but not the N.U.R., the railways operate a skeleton service with N.U.R. drivers.

Each union has its hierarchy of local and district organisations. Any member may attend the meetings of his local branch, but only a very small number of enthusiasts do attend. In unions which elect their officers at meetings, three-quarters or more of the members do not vote. Members' subscriptions, often £10 to £20 a year, are used to provide benefits for the members and to build up strike-funds; also to pay the salaries of full-time union officials, for the upkeep of office-buildings, and for the running expenses including journeys on union business. Most unions are affiliated to the Labour Party, and pay a small part of their members' subscriptions to the Party, which derives nearly all its money from this source. If a union member does not want to support the Labour Party in this way he may ask to 'contract out' of this 'political levy'.

A union member belongs to the branch based on the place where he lives, not on his factory. Branch, district and national spokesmen negotiate with associations of employers about pay and conditions. Within factories there are shop stewards, who negotiate with the immediate managements. They are often much concerned with the organisation of shift-working and with the effects of the introduction of new machines or processes. Even in the times of full employment, between roughly 1950 and 1965, some managements complained that they were discouraged from bringing in new technology or rationalisation of production to reduce the number of workers needed for a given level of output. That discouragement became greater in the 1970s.

When negotiations fail, union leaders may call upon their members to strike, go slow or 'work to rule'. The generic term 'industrial action' has come into use to describe unions' interference with the production process in furtherance of their own members' immediate wishes.

In most recent years the number of work-days lost through strikes has been less in Britain than in Italy, Canada or some other countries, but a strike of a few workers essential to a complxex process of production may make far more others idle and cause serious disruption. One special type of problem comes from 'unofficial' strikes, such as those called by shop stewards in workshops in particular factories, without any serious attempts having been made to settle the differences from which they arise.

For many years past opinion polls have shown that a majority of

British people have been unhappy about the organisation of trade unions. Even the majority of union members think the unions have too much power, and that the power is not well used. In 1969 the Labour Government produced a plan which they called *In Place of Strife*. The plan included definitions of the scope of union activity, many of which had long been generally accepted in other European countries. In particular, no strike should be called until processes of negotiation had been tried and failed to bring agreement. The plan produced a serious division within the Labour Party. Union leaders insisted that union officials must remain free to act without such restrictions. Many Labour M.P.s agreed with them. The government abandoned the plan, and Trades Union Congress promised that the unions would regulate their own behaviour, avoiding obvious abuses. But the T.U.C. had no real power, and popular disappointment over non-fulfilment of its promise probably contributed to the Conservative victory at the general election of 1970.

In 1970–71 the Conservative government brough in legislation partly resembling the proposals of *In Place of Strife*. But their law was passed against the objections of the unions, and by this time, being in opposition, the Labour Party fully supported their objections.

In retrospect, these events of 1969–70 seem to have marked an important turning point in British politics. Until then both of the major parties, at least when in power, had worked hard to achieve a degree of consensus among the major interests.

Anxious to restrain inflation the Conservative government also took power by law to restrict wage increases to fixed percentages. Late in 1973, when Europe's oil supplies from the Middle East were suddenly reduced, and Britain had a sudden need of more coal, the miners demanded a wage increase which seemed far beyond the legal limits. When this was not given, they first restricted production, then went on strike, supported by the Labour Party. Power supplies were cut. Factories could work only three days a week. The Conservative Prime Minister, Edward Heath, believing that public opinion supported his party, called an election in February 1974; this, as we have seen, put Labour in power.

The new Labour government tried to give the unions all they wanted. Fast-rising wages and prices quickly sent inflation to an annual rate of 30 per cent, with imports vastly exceeding exports. For a time the unions in general kept their further wage demands within some guidelines set by the government, but in 1978–9 a new wave of strikes contributed to the Labour government's down-fall in May 1979.

With the Conservatives in power, and Mrs Thatcher as Prime Minister, the government did not restrict wage increases, except in the public sector. With market forces operating, firms were forced to give high priority to efficiency. They demonstrated that big pay increases would drive them out of business; many reduced their staffs. As unemployment rose, so union membership fell.

The need for competitiveness was understood, and in 1981–3 fewer working days were lost through strikes than for many years. In the public sector industries the government insisted that public money provided for investment should be well used, and there was industrial action in protest against the closure of inefficient plants. Meanwhile, relations between the unions and the government remain hostile.

4   The Changing Structure of Work

The shape of British industry has changed enormously. In 1900 coal mining, textiles, shipbuilding and heavy engineering were its foundations; all these began to decline in the 1920s. They are located mainly in the north, Wales and Scotland, and the decline has been bad for those regions. In 1900 nearly a million men worked in the coalmines and produced 250 million tons of coal a year. By 1984 there were fewer than 200,000 miners, producing 120 million tons—though the miners' wages in this nationalised industry were well above the general average, and their living conditions incomparably better than those of the previous generation. Britain was producing a tiny proportion of the world's new ships, instead of more than half. The textile industry was greatly reduced. The steel industry, nationalised, denationalised then nationalised again, had not modernised itself effectively until after 1980.

Since the 1930s British industrial growth has been concentrated on newer industries: chemicals, electrical goods, vehicles, furniture and other consumer-durables. Much of the new development was in the midlands and the south, and even in the 1950s and 1960s, there was more unemployment in the north, and in Wales and Scotland. Government policies encouraged the new industries to build their factories in these old areas of declining heavy industry, but these policies had only moderate success.

By the 1970s some of the newer industries in their turn were suffering from the competition of more efficient foreign producers. Most cameras, refrigerators and washing machines were imported, and in 1977 half the new cars sold in Britain came from the European continent or Japan. The only significant British-owned car-producer, British Leyland, became insolvent in 1975 and was effectively taken over by the state, with no prospect of covering its real costs by sales for several years to come. Its commercial vehicle section and some of its high-quality products, particularly Land-Rover and Jaguar, were still successful, but its mass-production sections were overtaken, not only by foreign rivals but also by Ford's British operations.

After 1977 the downward trend in almost all kinds of manufacturing industries continued, and the decline was accentuated in 1979–82. In spite of a slow improvement in the production by each worker, the total amount produced declined, not only in the basic industries such as steel, but in machine tools and most kinds of manufacturing. Less than half as many new houses were started in 1981 as in 1976, though building of new offices continued. Then, in 1982–84, there was a slight increase, not only in productivity but in the total level of production, which returned to the level of 1979. With some gain in efficiency, companies which had made losses returned to profitability, even the mainly nationalised British Leyland. For the first time for many years productivity in British industry improved at a rate faster than the German. This was hardly yet a recovery, but at least ground for optimism.

In contrast to industry, British agriculture has been consistently almost the most efficient in Europe. The typical farmer is a tenant of an estate, working alone or with one or two employees, but equipped with ample tools and tractors which he knows how to use and maintain. With only two per cent of the labour force British agriculture can produce most of the food that Britain needs, and its output has grown by half in twenty years.

The industries which have grown, in numbers of people employed, are banking, finance, insurance, the calculation of liabilities to tax, the Law, public administration including physical planning and the adjudication of disputes, advertising, educational, health and social welfare services, and other functions not involving the production of goods for use. Four million people were employed in these in 1960, eight million in 1980. A large proportion of the people in these employments work for central or local government. Many of these new non-manual jobs demand a high level of education, and until 1980 this expansion, as well as the increase in the demand for skill in industry, kept pace with the growth in the number of young people spending longer in full-time education.

The great increase in non-manual jobs has been accompanied by an increase in the number of married women who go out to work—but husbands do not do a great deal more housework than before. Two factors have increased the number of women able to work: the decline in the size of families and the increase in convenience foods, in washing machines, vacuum cleaners and such appliances which reduce the time spent on housework. Only one family in five has more than two children; for most women without young children to look after, life at home and shopping are unsatisfying. Even some with small children would like to work, if the children could be cared for during mothers' working hours.

But the social and economic system has failed badly at several points to give scope for women. A working wife still does most of the food-buying, cooking and housework, and thus has less leisure than her husband. Hardly any households employ domestic servants and few women work as servants. There are few public nurseries and nursery-schools, and their hours of work and holiday closures are not well-adapted to the needs of working mothers. Part-time jobs with suitable hours are available, but few part-time jobs can fit in with a progressive career. The principle of equal pay for equal work has been accepted, but jobs done normally by women are badly paid, and the male-dominated trade unions are not helpful. Relatively few women are promoted to highly-paid positions. A quarter of all doctors are women, but nearly all the chief posts in hospitals are held by men. Slightly fewer women (4%) are in the House of Commons than in most European parliaments. The first woman was admitted to the Stock Exchange in 1972. About that time the average earnings of women in full-time work began to be equal to half of men's average earnings, and by 1978 the ratio had risen to nearly three-quarters.

Modern times have produced an active Women's Liberation Movement, apart from less strident pressure for better conditions of life and work for women. In 1975 the Equal Opportunities Commission was set up to protect and promote women's interests, and to keep under review the operation of the Sex Discrimination Act. Meanwhile, as affluence rises, women take more and more of the private decisions about the running of their households and the spending of the family's money. They also play a leading part outside the home in many of the pressure groups which are becoming steadily more influential. The scope of their traditional role is advancing more quickly than their economic and professional success.

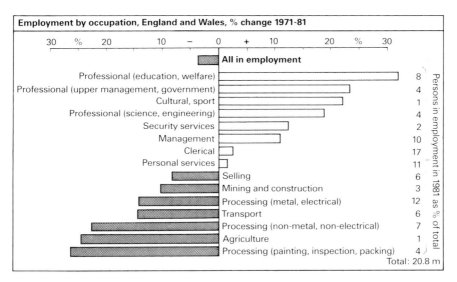

Employment by occupation, England and Wales, % change 1971-81

Occupation	Persons in employment in 1981 as % of total
All in employment	
Professional (education, welfare)	8
Professional (upper management, government)	4
Cultural, sport	1
Professional (science, engineering)	4
Security services	2
Management	10
Clerical	17
Personal services	11
Selling	6
Mining and construction	3
Processing (metal, electrical)	12
Transport	6
Processing (non-metal, non-electrical)	7
Agriculture	1
Processing (painting, inspection, packing)	4

Total: 20.8 m

Question

How much 'unproductive' work can a modern society afford?

Unemployment rates: by region

	percentages		
	1976	1979	1982
Standard regions			
North	7.2	8.3	16.5
Yorkshire and Humberside	5.3	5.4	13.4
East Midlands	4.5	4.4	11.0
East Anglia	4.7	4.2	9.9
South East	4.0	3.4	8.7
South West	6.2	5.4	10.8
West Midlands	5.5	5.2	14.9
North West	6.7	6.5	14.7
England	5.1	4.8	11.6
Wales	7.1	7.3	15.6
Scotland	6.7	7.4	14.2
Great Britain	5.4	5.2	12.1
Northern Ireland	9.5	10.8	19.4
United Kingdom	5.5	5.3	12.2

Question

Can you relate these figures to the industrial structure of Britain?

Supporters enjoying a football match.

7

Leisure and Private Life

1 Holidays

Attitudes to leisure have been much influenced by the modern love of moving around and by the ease of travel. Industrial workers have at least three weeks' holiday with pay each year, most professional workers a month or more. Factory holidays are concentrated in the period between mid-July and mid-August, and those who look for rationalisation are always wishing that the annual holiday could be spread over a longer period; but to make this convenient it would be necessary to make some changes in the school holidays too. State schools usually only have six weeks off in summer, from about mid-July to the end of August.

The coast is the most popular objective of English people for their annual holiday, but there are few new seaside hotels. Food in British hotels and restaurants is reasonably cheap, but rooms are not. Few English people rent houses or flats for their holidays, but one of the traditional ways of spending a summer holiday is in a boarding-house, which may have a card in its window advertising 'bed and breakfast'. In seaside towns there are whole streets of houses almost every one of which has such a notice in its window. Some boarding-house keepers provide all meals (board residence) for their guests, others provide breakfast only.

Camp-sites are regulated but not owned by local authorities. Most are farmers' fields, used by cows in the winter. British campers are realistic enough to recognise that caravans give better shelter than tents against the worst summer weather, but the caravans do not improve the scenery. Also they are a nuisance both when being pulled along the road and when stored for eleven months of the year beside their owners' garages. Some holidaymakers prefer to hire static caravans or chalets in 'holiday camps', of which the biggest are really self-contained holiday towns, with organised mass-entertainment as part of their attraction. Billy Butlin was the pioneer in developing mass holiday camps, mainly after 1945, and Butlin's camps are a national institution—soon followed by another organisation, Pontin's, whose camps are smaller and less organised.

The motor car, good roads and the decline in the farming population have recently encouraged town people to buy unwanted cottages in the country villages, and in the past ten years the competition for these houses has caused their price to rise so much that local people cannot buy them when they need to. Weekends at the country cottage are common even in winter, but owners often let them in summer.

The British may be conservative about the times at which they take their holidays, but they have shown themselves very ready to take to new places. They have always been pioneers in travelling far away, and Englishmen were among the first to climb many of the great Alpine summits. Now foreign travel is within reach of most working people, and each year more English men, women and children become familiar with some part of continental Europe. Many take their cars, often with tents or caravans, crossing the Channel by ferry or hovercraft or by car-carrying aeroplane; others use the travel agents' schemes for group travel and hotel booking, some of them, regrettably, being taken to hotels which have been trained to provide English food. Some, when they are away, become obsessed with the shops and devote much energy to thinking what to buy, struggling to convert the prices into English pounds and pence. When they get home again they talk endlessly of these things, boasting of their bargains and complaining of what they were asked to pay for cups of tea.

2   Sport

The English are great lovers of competitive sports; and when they are neither playing nor watching games they like to talk about them, or when they cannot do that, to think about them.

The game peculiarly associated with England is cricket. Many other games too are English in origin, but have been adopted with enthusiasm in other countries; but cricket has been seriously and extensively adopted only in the Commonwealth, particularly in Australia, India, Pakistan and the West Indies. So a liking for cricket seems to go along with an English spirit and attitude and with English institutions. It thrives in South Africa too.

Organised amateur cricket is played between club teams, mainly on Saturday afternoons. Nearly every village, except in the far north, has its cricket club, and there must be few places in which the popular image of England, as sentimentalists like to think of it, is so clearly seen as on a village cricket-field. A first-class match, as played between English counties, lasts for up to three days, with six hours' play on each day. The game is thus indeed slow, and a spectator, sitting in the afternoon sun after his lunch of sandwiches and beer, may be excused for having a little sleep for half an hour.

Cricket is making no progress in popularity. If cricket expresses and embodies the spirit of England, perhaps England is losing its spirit a little. For the great mass of the British public the eight months of the football season are more important than the four months of cricket. There are plenty of amateur association football (or 'soccer') clubs, but professional football is big business. Every large town has at least one professional football club. The players have not necessarily any personal connection with the town for whose team they play.

The annual Cup Final match, between the two teams which have defeated their opponents in each round of a knock-out contest, dominates the scene; the regular 'league' games, organised in four divisions, provide the main entertainment through the season and the basis for the vast system of betting on the football pools. More than half of the graffiti on public walls are aggressive statements of support for football teams, and the hooliganism of some British supporters has become notorious outside as well as inside Britain. The few intellectuals who are football enthusiasts thereby identify themselves in some degree with the working class.

Rugby football (or 'rugger') is played with an egg-shaped ball, which may be carried and thrown (but not forward). If a player is carrying the ball he may be 'tackled' and made to fall down. Each team has fifteen players, who spend much time lying in the mud or on top of each other and become very dirty, but do not need to wear such dramatic protective clothing as men playing American football. There is some professional League rugby in the north, but elsewhere rugby union is played by amateurs and favoured by the middle class. It is also the game played at the great majority of 'public schools', though more and more state schools are adopting it. International matches, involving England, Wales, Scotland, Ireland and France, are played in capital cities with crowds of up to

80,000, but a match between two first-class clubs may be watched by only a few dozen spectators. There are hundreds of amateur rugby clubs, many of them formed by 'old boys', or former pupils, of particular schools.

Most secondary schools have playing fields, and boys normally play rugger or soccer in winter and cricket in summer as a normal school activity; schoolgirls play tennis and rounders (a sort of baseball) in summer and netball and hockey in winter—though hockey is now becoming more and more popular also at boy's schools, and there are many men's amateur hockey clubs. Men's basketball is played by a tiny minority.

The more social adult games of golf and tennis are played by great numbers of people. Golf courses (together with the bars in their club houses) are great meeting places of the business community; it is, for example, very desirable for bank managers to play golf. There are plenty of tennis clubs, but most towns provide tennis courts in public parks, and anyone may play tennis cheaply on a municipal court. The courts are often empty. There are cheap municipal golf courses in Scotland but few in England. The ancient game of bowls is played, much more sedately than in southern France, mainly by middle-aged people, on reserved level stretches of beautifully-kept grass, often in municipal parks.

Next to Association Football, the chief spectator sport in English life is horse racing. Partly because of the laws which forbid such activities on Sundays, horse racing is organised rather differently in England from other countries. Each of the 63 race courses has from two to about six 'meetings' every year, with each meeting consisting of two, three or four consecutive days of racing; most horse racing takes place on working days and during working hours. There are totalisators at the race courses, but bookmakers are also allowed, and in each spectators' enclosure there is a long line of bookmakers offering their odds against the horses. Associated bookmakers in different enclosures employ 'tic-tac men' who communicate miraculously by private semaphore-type signalling systems.

Both horse and dog racing provide a means for betting; but with horse racing nine-tenths of the betting is done by post or at betting shops. There are horse races on at least one of Britain's race courses on every day of the year (weather permitting), and each day people take workers' bets from factories to the betting shops, just as they did to the flourishing illegal bookmakers before their activities were made legal in 1961. One-tenth of all men bet regularly on the races, and in 1976 they lost between them on average £200 each, or about 6% of average take-home pay.

Gambling in various forms is a major national pastime. Two-fifths of the adult population gamble regularly. In 1976 the 'true turnover' of the five main types of gambling (that is, the total net losses of those betting) was £800 million, of which the state took £300 million in betting taxes. Bets on horse and dog racing accounted for half of the total. Half of all British households stake on average £20 a year each on the football pools, which are the most foolish form of betting, because only 30% of the total staked is returned in prizes; the other 70% is divided between the state, through taxes, and the operators, whose administrative costs are high. The attraction of the pools is the remote possibility of an enormous win. Three million people, mainly women, go regularly to bingo sessions (often in old cinemas) where they enjoy the company as well as the prospect of some small success. But bingo is a very small operation; the 'true turnover', or net amount lost, on slot machines and casinos is fifteen times as great, and exceeds even that of the football pools. In 1978 a report of a Royal Commission on gambling (from which these figures are derived) showed that the community as a whole spent real resources worth £500 million on the operation of gambling devices, or about the same as it spent on University education. Nearly all gamblers lose in the long run. They include a small proportion of the very rich, a few of whom do themselves serious harm; but the vast majority are relatively poor, manual workers or unemployed or retired—though there are probably fewer than in the past to whom it becomes a dangerous obsession.

The general public like races of horses and dogs because these provide suitable pretexts for betting. Contests between human beings, in running or walking or jumping or throwing javelins or heavy weights, are less popular. The first properly-organised Olympic Games of the modern era were those held in London in 1908, but athletics have not gained much sustained public interest or support in Britain. The few star British runners, jumpers, etc., who achieve international success enjoy some public renown with the help of television and the press.

The 1980s have brought an increased interest in running, or jogging, for the sake of fitness, and huge numbers of people apply to take part in the many local marathon races. Britain has shared a little in the pursuit of gymnastics, made popular by eastern Europeans, but classes in aerobics, dancing and keep-fit exercises have a wider appeal. Since 1974 there has been a Minister for Sport, with the task of promoting development of facilities for all kinds of sports. One of his functions is to secure funds to cover the costs involved in training and travel for athletes who have potential for international competition. Also, with help from the central government, many towns have built new centres for sport and recreation, with gymnasia, swimming pools, squash courts and equipment, along with coaching staff.

Remarkably few people are interested in bicycle racing. On the other hand, rowing, in fours or eights, occupies a leading place in the sporting life of schools and universities which have suitable water near by, and several regattas, held mainly in summer are great social occasions, watched from the river banks by vast crowds of spectators.

When English people use the word 'hunting' they usually mean fox-hunting, a sport which is popular among a small but important minority. There are packs of hounds all over the country, and a 'meet', with the hunt all gathered together ready to start, many of the male riders wearing 'pink' (that is, red coats), is a colourful spectacle. Many of the horses are brought to the meet in vans, and on the whole hunting is a sport for the rich. A Master of Fox Hounds has a position of much honour. There are some people who would like to see fox-hunting forbidden by law on the ground that it is cruel, but there is little likelihood that this will be done. The Royal Society for the Prevention of Cruelty to Animals recognises that other methods of killing foxes, such as shooting and trapping, may be more cruel than hunting. It includes enthusiastic fox-hunters among its most generous and socially-eminent supporters, and is not inclined, as a body, to take steps against hunting. But it has an anti-hunting left wing.

Americans use the word 'hunting' to include the shooting of birds, but the English do not. The moorlands of the north and of Scotland are rich in grouse and partridge, and to go shooting on the moors is perhaps the most distinctive of upper-class activities.

People do not shoot or trap ordinary wild birds for sport. When English people hear of such practices in Italy or France, they are horrified. Fishing is the most popular participatory sport of all, either simply and cheaply in nearby water or expensively in one of the Scottish rivers which are specially stocked with trout or salmon.

England was the first home of many of the modern world's most popular sports. The English cannot claim, today, that they have, as a nation, surpassing skill in any form of sport when they engage in international competition. But they care strongly about the 'sporting spirit', the capacity to play with respect for the rules and the opponents, to win with modesty and to lose with good temper. One sometimes hears people talking as though 'sportsmanship' were a peculiarly English quality. To make such claims, even to think them justified, may itself be unsportsmanlike, but at least it can probably be said with justice that the English are very strong in their adherence to the theory of sportsmanship, and are ashamed of the recent behaviour of some football mobs.

3 Theatre and Cinema

The theatre is mainly concentrated in London, where there are at least forty theatres functioning, and a successful play can continue to run for many months or even years. Outside London a few large towns have theatres in which are performed, generally for one week at a time, plays which take a trial run before opening in London, or which have completed periods of being shown in London.

The term 'repertory' used to describe a fairly small theatre at which the same company put on a fresh play every week. Most towns have such theatres, but the pattern has become more varied. Some provincial theatres are connected with Arts Centres, and are ready to be experimental, catering for minority tastes, often subsidised by the Arts Council and by private subscription. One of the main British theatres is the Shakespeare Memorial Theatre at Stratford; there is also a magnificent and distinguished theatre at Chichester, in West Sussex. Training in drama has developed enormously, and there are now academic Departments of Drama in some universities. The old music-hall, or variety theatre, is dead, but is revived in the form of Christmas pantomimes which occupy big theatres for several weeks.

Orchestral concerts are given regularly in London by several first-class orchestras which are based there. In the later part of the summer there is each night a 'promenade concert' at the Royal Albert Hall, with the seats taken out from the floor of the hall, so as to allow a very large number of people to hear the concerts standing in the 'promenade', with a low charge for admission. The largest provincial centres also maintain permanent orchestras, which give regular concerts. All these orchestras occasionally visit other places to give concerts, and some financial help is given to them by the Arts Council or by local authorities. The Royal Opera House at Covent Garden, in central London, is leased by the government to the Covent Garden Opera House Trust, which receives a government grant. Seasons of opera are performed there and also of ballet by the Royal Ballet, which has in recent years been one of the most successful of British ventures in the Arts.

Touring opera and ballet companies visit the principal theatres in major towns. Opera of the highest quality is performed throughout every summer at Glyndebourne, 90 kilometres south of London but visited by people who come from London and its suburbs.

Local enterprise has been responsible for the development in recent years of 'festivals' of the arts in several places, of which the best known is the annual International Festival of Music and Drama in Edinburgh, held late in August each year. As well as the performances by musicians, etc. from all over the world, the 'fringes' of the Festival produce an interesting variety of plays by less established companies. Among other such festivals are those held at Bath, Aldeburgh (in Suffolk, connected with Benjamin Britten), Pitlochry in the Scottish Highlands and Llangollen in north-central Wales. The Three Choirs Festival, which circulates among the three western cathedral cities of Gloucester, Worcester and Hereford, has a continuous history going back to 1724.

From about 1930 until very recent times the cinema enjoyed an immense popularity in Britain, and the palatial cinemas built in the 1930s were the most impressive of the buildings to be seen in the streets of many towns. More recently the rapid spread of television has brought a great change. In 1946 the average British person went to the cinema forty times in the year, but by 1982 the figure had fallen to 1.2 times, and 1,500 cinemas were closed during this period. Most films shown are from Hollywood, but some British films have won great international success. For French and other foreign-language films there is a healthy prejudice against 'dubbed' English sound-tracks, and such films are usually shown with English sub-titles.

The ownership of cinemas is highly concentrated, and many of the abandoned cinemas are now used as bingo-halls. Some surviving cinemas now show mainly horror or sex films, and in some towns films mainly for the benefit of immigrants from India.

Others, including the biggest and (outside London) a few new ones, have survived by showing 'big' feature films. Arts Centres and Cinema Clubs show films, including old ones, in small halls, often three in one building.

Censorship of the theatre 'for the preservation of good manners, decorum and the public peace' was at last abolished in 1968, but the cinema is subject to a form of censorship. The censorship of films has been so relaxed that it has almost disappeared, except for the classification of some films as unsuitable for children.

4   Other Recreations

Visitors to provincial England sometimes find the lack of public activities in the evenings depressing. There are, however, many activities which visitors do not see. Evening classes, each meeting usually once a week, are flourishing immensely, and not only those which prepare people for examinations leading to professional qualifications. Many people attend classes connected with their hobbies, such as photography, painting, folk-dancing, dog-training, cake-decoration, archaeology, local history, car maintenance and other subjects, some of them no less surprising than some of these. The classes may be organised by the local education authority or by the Workers' Educational Association, and in them people find an agreeable social life as well as the means of pursuing their own hobbies more satisfactorily. All this, together with the popularity of amateur dramatics, can provide some comfort for those who fear that modern mass entertainment is producing a passive society.

Apart from the organised classes, mention must also be made of the groups which meet regularly for a mixture of social and religious purposes under the auspices of churches of various denominations, and of the privately-arranged groups of people who join together for the pursuit of their hobbies. For young people there are many youth clubs, some but not all of them connected with churches, which perform a very useful function; but it must be said that, particularly in towns, there are teenage groups or gangs which prefer pastimes of a more negative kind, however hard club-organisers try to meet them halfway.

Great numbers of people, especially women of middle class and middle age, spend much of their leisure time working together for good causes, making clothes or food or collecting money for the benefit of the various types of people who are in need, and some of this good work is now co-ordinated with services provided by the public authorities. All of this demands a good deal of organisation and innumerable committees. Most of it needs money, and the workers for good causes spend much time in trying to extract funds from the rest of the community to supplement the subscriptions which they pay themselves. Subject to the regulations made by the public authorities and with their permission, the supporters of a good cause may organise a 'flag-day', normally not more than once a year in any town. They stand in the streets with collecting boxes into which generously disposed passers-by put money, receiving in exchange little paper 'flags' to pin on their coats. Other devices are 'bazaars' or 'sales of work', with opening speeches made by persons of importance. All these activites turn out to be social occasions. In the course of doing good the public-spirited develop their social lives, meet their friends and enjoy themselves.

Public libraries, maintained by the local authorities, are very well developed and progressive, and everywhere allow people to borrow books without charge. The books in the lending section are always kept on open shelves, and library staffs are very helpful in getting books on request from other libraries through the exchange system. Most libraries report an increase in borrowing over the past few years, so television does not seem to be stopping people from reading, as it was feared that it would. Many towns have well and imaginatively-kept museums and art galleries.

England is famous for its gardens, and most people like gardening. This is probably one reason why so many people prefer to live in houses rather than flats. Particularly in suburban areas it is possible to pass row after row of ordinary small houses, each one with its neatly-kept patch of grass surrounded by a great variety of flowers and shrubs. Some people who have no gardens of their own have patches of land or 'allotments' in specially reserved areas. Enthusiasts at gardening—or at do-it-yourself activities—get ever-growing help from radio programmes, magazines and patient shop-keepers.

Although the task of keeping a garden is so essentially individual, gardening can well become the foundation of social and competitive relationships. Flower-shows and vegetable-shows, with prizes for the best exhibits, are immensely popular, and to many gardeners the process of growing the plants seems more important than the merely aesthetic pleasure of looking at the flowers or the prospect of eating the vegetables. Quite often a competitive gardener's ambition is to grow the biggest cabbages or leeks or carrots, and the plain fact that the merits of most vegetables on the table are in inverse ratio to their size seems often to be forgotten. But the English have never had much reputation for their appreciation of good food or good cooking.

Dancing is popular, and the numerous large and opulent-looking public dance-halls are an important element in the folklore and courtship procedures of all but the upper and middle classes. They manage to survive against the competition of the more modern, smaller, noisier discothéques. Lately nightclubs have spread from London to other towns, and in the north some old workmen's clubs are now almost indistinguishable from sophisticated nightclubs.

Dinner out in a restaurant in the evening is a rare event in the provinces, though becoming less rare as the food improves—and there really has been a big improvement since 1960. Unfortunately the public give too little encouragement to good cooks and are too tolerant of bad ones. Hotel dining-rooms are used mainly by people who are spending the night, and by groups and associations which are not much concerned with the quality of the food.

A special British institution is the fish and chip shop, where it is possible to buy over the counter a piece of fried fish and potatoes. You can eat the fish and chips in the street as you walk along, or take it home, if you live near by, and eat it on a plate. Now the traditional fish and chips is supplemented by other kinds of hot food to take away and eat at home, including roast chicken and a huge variety of Indian curries and Chinese dishes, packed in elegant containers instead of the old newspapers of the traditional fish and chip shop. Another way of eating at home, without cooking, is to buy ready-to-eat convenience foods at grocers' shops and supermarkets. The working housewife does not need to spend too long in the kitchen when she returns home.

Everywhere there are plenty of pubs, in which people play darts, talk and drink, usually while standing up. A few old pubs have real character and a few new ones have a certain streamlined comfort, but many are dull and ugly, their walls decorated with dismal notices saying that no betting is allowed and no young person may be served with drinks. It seems that the English think it rather indecent for people to drink alchoholic drinks in any place where they can be seen from outside; so pubs usually not only have no tables outside, but are so built that it is impossible for people outside to see in, or for those who are inside to see out. There are a few exceptions to this, mostly in the south, but not many. The traditional pub was a place for the men only. But things have changed, and more and more pubs are now places where men and women sit at tables, and they often provide good lunches.

The notorious British drinking laws are full of absurdities. They cause plenty of irritation, but probably do not reduce the amount of drinking. Perhaps this is the reason why the drink trade itself seems little interested in attempts to get the laws radically changed. A reform promised for 1961 has turned out to be no real reform at all. Alcoholic drinks, including beer, are allowed to be sold in any place for only nine hours each day; it is for the local Justices of the Peace to decide exactly what those hours should be. In the provinces they are often from 11 a.m. until 3 p.m., and from 5.30 p.m. until 10.30 p.m. In some places, including London, 11 p.m. is the 'closing time'. Special rules apply to clubs, and special exemptions from the normal rules may be granted by magistrates for particular occasions. Again, drinks may only be sold in establishments licensed for the sale of drink, and in practice these are either hotels or pubs, or licensed grocers or wine merchants which sell bottles to take away. Cheap restaurants rarely have licences to sell drink, even beer.

The laws restricting the hours of drinking in public places go back to the sharp political arguments of the late nineteenth century, when the Liberal Party had a strong policy for restriction. In the 1870s British people were the biggest drinkers in the world, but later they became more abstemious than most other Europeans. In the 1930s alcoholism was not a serious problem, but from 1950 there was a new increase, due partly to the fairly small increase in the tax on drinks. In 1950 a bottle of whisky cost, including tax, half the average weekly wage, in 1984 only a twentieth. This, with massive advertising, may have encouraged people to drink more. In 1968 new laws enabled courts to take away the driving licence of a driver who was found to have more than 80 ml. of alcohol, but the pubs are surrounded by visiting cars at 10 p.m. Serious alcoholic illness has for the first time become prevalent among women— perhaps because it is now so easy to buy liquor in supermarkets.

There is a strong tradition of hospitality, and most entertaining in people's homes is free and easy, informal, and without rituals. The old afternoon tea-party has lost popularity, even on Sundays, partly because few people dare to eat the scones, butter and jam and cakes which go with the traditional English tea. Friends and relations are asked instead, two or four or thirty at a time, for drinks before lunch or dinner, or for a meal which nowadays is often a buffet supper eaten with difficulty away from the table.

5 Marriage, Home and Family

The mid-twentieth century has brought three great and obvious changes: contraception, personal mobility, and a concern for the equality of women. Along with these, and joining them together, we have a value-system which rejects the idea that anyone is superior to anyone else, and hence a rejection of established authority except that which arises within a self-conscious peer-group. Old accepted patterns of behaviour, including courtship and the ways by which male and female met, have withered away, and have been replaced by nothing definable.

At home parents do not restrict the movements of their children. The older dance-halls, and the newer noisy discothéques, are still places where young people meet, but other acceptable opportunities are so numerous and so easy that it is pointless to attempt to list or discuss them. Girls expect to go to work when they finish their education, no matter at what age between 16 and 23. They meet men at work, within their peer-group and through their parents' friends. One girl forms a stable relationship with a boy early, another has several 'boy-friends' in succession. Most have sex before marriage. Most are successful in avoiding unwanted pregnancy at this stage, some marry when they become pregnant. Increasing numbers of couples set up home without being married, though the vast majority marry before having children.

For those who become pregnant and are unable or unwilling to marry, abortion has been available, subject to restrictions, since 1967. The restrictions are not very precise, and their meaning depends mainly on the interpretations of individual medical practitioners. Even so, the number of legal abortions carried out in any year has not greatly exceeded 100,000, or only a small fraction of the number of illegal abortions in Italy under the severely restrictive Italian laws of the early 1970s. The main effect of the easing of the law has been enormously to reduce the incidence of bad effects on the health of the women. A large proportion of abortions are performed on married women who already have large families.

In one way the new acceptance of extra-marital sexual activity has been bad for the female; it is easier for a male to get his satisfaction without incurring any responsibility, and in a world where people are encouraged to think that they have a right to whatever they want, some girls suffer from being treated without the personal respect which older values expected males to show.

The vast majority of children are born to married couples, though a quarter of all women who marry are pregnant at the time. Half of all first marriages in recent years were before the age of 21. Half of all marriages are civil only, the other half religious; and the rituals surrounding marriage have become less elaborate and less rigid than in the past.

Most women who marry continue to go out to work until they have children, and few aspire to have more than two children. The birth rate declined in 1965–77 as in most other countries, and in 1977 was around the E.E.C. average at 12 per 1,000 population. There was some sign of a new increase in 1977–8; but this rise, caused partly by the high birth rate twenty years before, was not sustained into the 1980s.

Most women with very small children stay at home to look after them, unless they can make other arrangements. Few married couples live near to their own parents, and grandmothers are much inclined to go out to work themselves. There are not enough places in nursery-schools to provide for all the young mothers who would like to go to work, but a few work-places provide crèches, and there are private enterprise 'child-minders' registered with the local authorities, and a few who are (illegally) unregistered and uninspected. When the children are old enough to go to school their mothers are inclined to go out to work again sooner or later, often leaving children of ten years old to go home with their own latch-keys when they come out of school at 3.30 in the afternoon.

Parents have become more indulgent to their children in every way, giving them ample presents and money and not exercising much discipline. There is so much variety that generalisation is unwise, but serious misbehaviour, including vandalism, by young children, increased ten times over in twenty years, and is often blamed on weak parental control. The 'problem families' are well known to the huge army of social service workers, whose members increased as much as did the acts of wanton damage and other anti-social acts of children in this period.

In well-adjusted families modern life gives scope for more

collective family activity, helped by car and garden, and above all by the television set which can amuse all together. Improved housing has made family life more private, and with privacy has gone a decline in the informal social control of neighbours' opinions. While the nuclear family of parents and children has grown closer together (except where the children demand and take more independence), the extended family has become weaker. Young people, when they marry, tend to live well away from their parents and other relations, often in different towns; and many people in non-manual careers move from one town to another at intervals of five, ten or fifteen years, so that many children hardly know their aunts or cousins.

Left then to themselves, some nuclear families remain isolated, others find some sense of community by befriending people met at work or in some organised social group.

Whatever the reason, the nuclear family as an institution has not universally adapted itself to these recent changes. Until 1971 divorce was obtainable without much difficulty on the ground of 'matrimonial offence', but then a new law allowed divorce by agreement, defined as 'irretrievable breakdown of marriage'. When married people have difficulties they may ask for help and advice from local authority social service workers or from the unpaid counsellors of a private organisation, the Marriage Guidance Council. In spite of these efforts, the divorce rate doubled in ten years, and is now the highest in any European country except Denmark. About one-third of all marriages end in divorce, and a much smaller number in legal separation. The legal costs involved in divorce and separation are substantial, but often funded from the legal aid system, paid out of tax revenue. Meanwhile the number of couples who set up home together without marrying has increased enormously. It seems likely that before 1990 one child in ten will be living with a divorced parent, and one in thirty with an unmarried mother. The legal arrangements for a divorce or separation normally require the father to pay a weekly allowance to the mother, but not all fathers keep up their payments. Magistrates' courts spend much time on attempts to put pressure on defaulting fathers, but the ultimate sanction, prison, does not help anyone. Many children of divorced parents, as well as those of unmarried mothers, depend on social security payments for their support, and some of them also need help from the local authorities' social services.

The early age of marriage may well have led to an increase in the number of unsatisfactory homes, and the easier divorce laws allow people to escape from misery of one kind. In consequence there may now be more people who live miserable lives for other reasons.

The word 'permissiveness' is used to describe a characteristic of modern times. The laws allow actions which were once forbidden, and when people break the laws every effort is made to treat them as victims of circumstances rather than as wicked people deserving anger and punishment. Meanwhile the old social controls of religion, extended family and close-knit neighbourhood have been weakened. The new freedoms, along with the newly-available material goods, have created opportunities for freer and more varied living; and where they produce misery (for example, among the victims of individual anti-social acts) the public authorities have a vast and caring apparatus through which to help. And where the public authorities have not yet been active, spontaneous groups are formed, financed by private subscription, to cure evils which official action has ignored. The Marriage Guidance Council has been mentioned. There is also a well-organised group of counsellors ready to give advice and comfort by telephone to people who contemplate suicide. Probably fewer wives suffer violence from their husbands than in the rougher past. When they do suffer they have less protection from neighbours (who tend to want privacy and to respect the privacy of others) or their own extended families (who live far away); but groups of kindly people have bought houses as refuges for battered wives. Other groups exert pressure on the state to take action to eliminate unhappiness and discomfort in countless forms. The ideal of 'a caring society' is constantly preached, and not by words alone. To replace the old 'care' of neighbourhood and family (which was often intolerant and censorious) there is now a more widely diffused kind of 'caring' which begins on an impersonal basis and produces masses of statistics. The 'caring' extends to places and things as well as people; some groups are active for the preservation of public footpaths, or old buildings threatened by plans to widen streets or build new office-blocks, or for the elimination of lead from petrol, or for better public transport.

For many individuals and families who live far from their own cousins and aunts, involvement in these activities is an important part of their social role. The overall effect of all this work is highly positive; but in the long run, most of it leads to more demands for action by the state, which (at central or local level) is the ultimate arbiter and provider to the fields of physical planning and social services alike. Public participation in the affairs of the community has increased, and for many it is part of private life; but spontaneous participation by non–elected persons who work through groups demands an ever growing number of public officials; and private life, though subject to less neighbourly interference, has its conditions more regulated by forces which are in their nature impersonal.

Spectator sports in Britain		
	millions per year	
	1971-72	1982-83
Football	30	22
Rugby football	2	2
Horse racing	4	4
Greyhound racing	9	5
Motor sports	—	4
Cricket	1	0.8

People participating in sports in Britain		
	percentage	
	1977	1980
Outdoor		
Male	35	37
Female	21	23
Indoor		
Male	31	32
Female	12	15

Question

Does it surprise you that people in Britain seem to be engaging in sport more themselves, but watching it less?

Above: Old terraced houses.

Below: A new housing estate.

8

Houses, Cars
and Public Transport

More than half of British families own their homes, the others rent
them, mainly from their district councils. More than half own cars.
Home and travel are two subjects which absorb people's thoughts
and activity. Both are private, but in a crowded modern country
both depend on the policies of state and local government. The
planning of roads and streets, houses and factories and commercial
zones, occupies both local and central government more and more.
In 1970 Mr Heath, as Conservative Prime Minister, created in the
central government the Department of the Environment, and three
interconnected eighteen-storey towers were built near Westminster
to manage the government of these activities. In 1976 a separate
Department of Transport was hived off again, but it still occupies
the same tower as before. Political argument about all aspects of
activity affecting the environment became intense in the early
1970s, and public participation in the process of decision has grown,
with public enquiries enabling opponents to state their arguments
against proposed new developments of any kind. Fashions have
changed with bewildering speed. The changes have been reflected
in the ever-growing volume of structure-plans and documents for
consultation, produced by civil servants, professional planners and
specialist consultants as well as by private bodies like the Town and
Country Planning Association, the Chambers of Commerce and
the Council for the Protection of Rural England.

1   Housing

English people traditionally like to live in small houses, not
apartments (which they call 'flats'). The usual building material is
red brick. Houses built before 1910 were very often arranged in
long, uniform rows or terraces, with no gap between the houses,

and with each house containing a front room and a back room on each of its two floors, with perhaps a small room above the entrance hall. In central areas of towns some bigger houses had more floors, but even a house with four floors was usually on the same basic pattern, with a basement for servants and the top rooms for the children. Houses standing alone in their own grounds were normally very large, and until 1850, of very pleasing design. Another fairly widespread arrangement, for the moderately opulent, was the semi-detached house, usually still on the same basic arrangement, but with houses built in pairs and some space left between the pairs.

In the older type of small terrace or semi-detached house the family often tended to live entirely in the back room on the ground floor, and to keep the front room only for the purpose of receiving guests rather formally; though visiting brothers or sisters, and others to whom it was not necessary to give an impression of respectability, would still be received in the back room, which would contain the stove used for cooking—itself probably the only heating device actually operating during the winter. Many English people still live in houses of this type, but recent builders have shown more readiness to experiment. In the 1960s many local councils built blocks of flats fifteen to twenty storeys high, to save space. The new high buildings have been unpopular, and by 1973 this system had been abandoned. Most of the latest houses are small again, far from town centres and best reached by car.

If an English person has enough money and security, he will probably buy a house for himself to live in. A few people have houses built for themselves on pieces of land which they have bought, but most new houses for private ownership are built by speculative builders, often in rows of rather similar small villas, semi-detached or detached, in their small gardens and with garages. A typical family house has four principal rooms (70 to 100 square metres of floor space) with a small garden. Prices trebled in 1965–73, but then rose more slowly than the general rate of inflation.

To buy a house, a person does not usually need to have all the money himself to pay for it; there are house-purchase banks, called 'building societies', from which it is possible to borrow up to 90% of the value of the house on the security of the property. The building societies are obliged to change their rates of interest from time to time, and they also change their policy with regard to the lending of money, being sometimes strict and slow to lend money at all on old houses, at other times much more liberal. A typical borrower pays back a little of the loan on his house each year, so that in about twenty years it becomes his property. The interest on the loans varies. In 1974–6 it was above 10% per year, but then fluctuated. Local authorities may also give mortgages up to the full value of a house.

In England over 60 per cent of all families own the houses in which they live, and the proportion of owner-occupiers is increasing slowly but steadily—though many of these are still paying back their mortgages.

The position regarding houses for rent has been complicated in recent years by the intervention of the Government. The rows of red brick town houses built in the nineteenth century were mostly built by private enterprise for the purpose of being rented. Many of these were of very poor quality and often became overcrowded, and in the early twentieth century the principle was accepted that the public authorities should build houses and let them at less than the economic rent to people who needed such subsidies in order to enable them to live in conditions that would not be damaging to their health.

Since 1945 nearly half of all new houses or flats have been built by local (district) councils. Both the number and the proportion have fluctuated. In general when a local council is controlled by the Labour Party it is enthusiastic for building houses. Labour-controlled local councils are more vigorous than others in building houses, while others are readier to sell their existing houses to their tenants. Labour governments at the centre encourage and help local councils both to build and to keep the rents low with the help of subsidies. Changes of political majority have led to changes of policy, so there has been little continuity.

In most districts there are waiting lists of people hoping to have subsidised council houses or flats allocated to them, and the council officials fix the order of priority in accordance with principles determined by the council itself. Once a family has a council house its security of tenure continues even if its circumstances change.

About one-third of the population now live in council houses, but these include a quarter of the people with incomes at least 25% above the average, and only half of those who are 25% or more below the average. Council tenants, at any level of income, are more inclined to support the Labour Party, and to regard themselves as 'working class', than other people at the same income-levels, but in reality the council house system has moved a long way from its original conception.

By 1980 nearly all the nineteenth century slums had been cleared, replaced by new flats or houses, some on the slum clearance land, some on new green-field sites spreading outwards from the towns. On the criteria of numbers of rooms and space per person, and of basic amenities inside the house, Britain compares well with other countries. But there are new troubles. The high blocks of flats built by councils in the 1960s were unpopular. Too many had been let to families with children who spoiled the lifts, defaced the hallways and made life miserable for the other tenants. Then it was found that many new council houses (not only tower blocks) had been badly built. Some have had to be repaired at great expense, a few demolished after less than twenty years of use.

When Mrs Thatcher's government came into power in 1979 it soon promoted measures to give effect to the Conservative preference for private ownership. Central government subsidies to local authorities were drastically reduced, and new building of council houses soon fell to a quarter of the level of the mid-1970s. New legislation required councils to sell houses to tenants wishing to buy them; in 1982 200,000 houses were sold in this way and only 50,000 new ones built. New private building was encouraged, and in 1983 local planning authorities were advised to be less rigid than before in forbidding new construction on land designated as 'green belt'. The Conservatives also wanted to increase the flexibility of the market for rented houses. Rent controls and the tenants' security of tenure had discouraged private letting; these restrictions were relaxed, though not abolished.

By now the highest housing densities, and the highest proportion of private tenancies, are in a few central-city areas inhabited mainly by professional people. In the most fashionable parts of central London—Chelsea, Kensington and Hampstead—three-quarters of all households in 1974 were tenants paying rent to private landlords, compared with one-quarter in the east-end constituency of Stepney, where three-quarters were council tenants, with lower density. Except in a few small central areas of cities, with mobile populations, private landlords no longer exploit the poor as they once did. With rents strictly controlled, and tenures secure, the owners can now obtain grants from the local authorities towards the cost of improvements. Attempts are being made to rehabilitate those nineteenth century terraces which still survive, and some, as in Islington in north central London, are being 'gentrified'. Luxurious properties are not controlled; with the rest the landlords tend to sell their houses or flats when they have the opportunity. Some even keep them empty, rather than take in tenants who cannot be removed; but when they do this they run the risk of finding their empty houses occupied by squatters. The same thing can happen to empty houses belonging to local councils and other public authorities. Some owners are not displeased when this happens, and make amicable arrangements with the irregular tenants who do repairs, make themselves comfortable and pay no rent—and leave when they are asked to do so.

This new tolerance of a few irregular occupations of empty houses (or other buildings) reflects a general recognition that recent government policies, and change of policy, towards housing have not worked very well. In 1977 52,000 people were registered as homeless, and it was estimated that 800,000 houses were empty—most of them owned by councils and other public bodies. Seven years later both these figures had been reduced substantially, and there were fewer squatters. Meanwhile new private building had increased.

One interesting experiment was based on the New Towns Act of 1948. Fifteen existing small towns or villages, half of them in the south-east near London, the others about 30 to 50 kilometres from other major cities, were designated as new towns. Each had a development corporation independent of existing local authorities, and by the 1970s each of these had developed substantially, not just as one huge housing estate but as a full new community, with factories, shops and offices as well, and with a carefully planned system of local roads and transport. Later a dozen other new towns were designated, some based on quite large towns whose existing populations of 50,000 to 120,000 were expected to double fairly rapidly. This latest group, partly intended to cope with the population-growth which was expected in the south-east in the last years of this century, is now developing more slowly than was at first intended; but the new towns as a whole have, in general, been more successful than the less-planned new urbanisation of the fringes of towns.

Apart from the designated new towns, many of the old country villages within a radius up to 50 kilometres round the major cities are becoming urban dormitories. Middle class people with families are mainly responsible for buying and improving old village houses or building new houses on the edge of villages from which they make long daily journeys to their offices in town. In the south-east these daily 'commuting' journeys are mainly done by train. On the busiest of a dozen routes to London, that from mid-Sussex and its coast, including Brighton, 10,000 commuters travel by train between 50 and 120 kilometres each way between their country or seaside homes and their work. With other towns these commuters travel mostly by car, but even for them, journeys of 50 kilometres are quite common.

2   Cars and Roads

The British travel mostly in their cars: twelve times more person-kilometres by car than by train. For several decades until 1960 they had more cars per thousand people, and travelled more by car, than any other Europeans. Since then they have been overtaken by most of the other advanced European countries; nevertheless, in 1978 more than three-fifths of all British households had a car. The lowest car-ownership rates were in the biggest cities; the highest in the most rural areas (where life without a car has become difficult) and in the semi-rural zones surrounding large towns, particularly London.

The British have for fifty years been peculiarly inclined to admire and want very superior cars; not only big and luxurious ones but also cars which sacrifice comfort and utility to speed. The British motor-industry has been more successful in selling cars of these types to the world than in producing merely useful vehicles. Meanwhile, in Britain itself, it has become less easy than in the past to guess a person's status from his car.

Britain was slow in improving the road-system in the 1950s, but by 1984 the 3,000 kilometres of motorways covered all the main trunk routes. This was still only one-third of the length of motorways in West Germany, though the British road system also included a further 2,000 kilometres of dual carriageway roads, not classified as motorways. The road system was in general adequate, except in rush hours and on Saturdays in summer. New road-building, apart from local by-passes, was inhibited by growing concern about environmental damage.

Three-quarters of all freight-movement in Britain is carried by lorries—a far bigger proportion than in West Germany or France.

Car-drivers suffer from the results, particularly in southern England, where improvements to the road system have been much less generous than in the north.

Although the roads, particularly in the south, are less adequate for the traffic than in other countries of the E.E.C., the number of people killed in accidents (8,000 in 1965, 5,500 in 1983) is much smaller, in relation to the volume of traffic, than in France, West Germany or Benelux. Even so, it has been calculated that the cost of road-accidents in Britain is nearly 1% of the gross national product.

3   Public Transport

Travel by train is easy on the main routes radiating from London. The railways provide a service of at least one fast train per hour to each important town in England and South Wales. All the trains have two classes, and there is not much difference between first and second class, except in price. By 1978 the only electrified lines were London to Glasgow, local lines in the south-east and lines around Manchester and Glasgow, but in 1976 the railways began to introduce complete services of diesel trains running at 200 kilometres an hour, first on the route to Bristol and South Wales, followed in 1978 by the route to north-east England and Edinburgh.

There are good air services between London, Scotland and Ireland, Manchester and Newcastle, but few other internal air routes. International scheduled air services are almost all concentrated at London's main airport, Heathrow, which was from December 1977 at last served by the London underground railway system, by trains running through the Piccadilly tube every four to ten minutes. The other main London airport, Gatwick, has always been served by trains on the line between Brighton and Victoria, which is one of the ten London main-line railway stations.

In 1961 it was decided that a third new airport for London would be needed by the early 1970s. An inland site half-way to Cambridge was designated but eventually abandoned in the face of environmental opposition. In 1971 preparatory work began at Maplin Sands, in the Thames estuary 90 kilometres from London, but the Labour Government stopped the plan in 1974. It found that the existing London airports could handle traffic-growth until 1990. It also considered using one or more provincial airports to serve

some of London's needs; Birmingham's airport was, even then,
only 75 minutes by train from London. Such a scheme would have
helped the provincial airports, which are still used mainly by British
package-tours to the Mediterranean; they belong to local councils,
and most are subsidised by the local ratepayers. The aviation
interest did not like this idea, which was abandoned—though not
irrevocably—in 1978.

The London and Scottish airports are owned by the British
Airports Authority, the main airlines by another nationalised
corporation, British Airways—though there are also some private
airlines. Aircraft-manufacture was first subsidised, then taken over,
by the State. The biggest subsidy of all has gone to the
technological achievement, the Concorde, which by 1979 had
enabled a few thousand privileged persons to make some flights in
four hours instead of seven.

The problems of transport in towns, and the rapid changes in the
conventional wisdom about solutions, typify the uncertainty with
which people accommodate themselves to the speed of change. The
last trams were removed many years ago, soon to be followed by
electric trolley-buses, which had a short-lived vogue. Apart from
the railway-systems of London, Glasgow, Liverpool and Tyneside,
buses provide the main public transport in towns. The top deck of a
double-decker bus is a good place from which to see the view, but
efficient bus-operation is not helped by the crude system of fare-
payment. Each passenger pays the fare, which depends on the
length of each particular journey, in cash to the conductor, who
walks round selling tickets to people in their seats. There is usually
no suitable space where passengers can stand if the bus is full, and
once the bus has about five standing passengers others are turned
away. If there is no conductor, passengers pay the fare as they get in.

Cars, ever more numerous, get in each others' way both when
travelling and when looking for places to park. Bus services,
suffering from the congestion, are slow and unreliable, and they
have fewer passengers. By 1960 every town had a twenty-year plan
for improving its road-system, and by 1970 some new urban roads
were already built or under construction. Since then a whole
profession of urban planners has grown up, dedicated to the
attempt not to repeat the mistakes of past generations. Millions of
pounds have been spent on the preparation of middle-term and
long-term plans for the structure of urban regions, including
housing, industry and commerce, along with provision for

movement. Since the mid-1970s these plans have been presented and discussed at public local meetings, attended by the most serious-minded citizens. Many of these, along with some professional planners, have lately been preaching the need to improve public transport for the benefit of people who have no access to a car. Central government funds have been used to contribute to local transport subsidies, but no area has yet introduced fares-free buses.

In 1974 the Nottingham Council, then dominated by the Labour Party, made a pioneering attempt to persuade car-owners to use buses when going to the central area. The plan was thoroughly and carefully worked out, but within a year it was judged to have been a failure.

In 1976–7 the activity of the previous years lost much of its momentum. A new and drastic need for economy took precedence

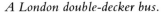
A London double-decker bus.

over new plans. Cars ceased to proliferate. In these two years the birth rate was so low that the population of England and Wales declined. So many forecasts for 1977, made in 1970, had turned out to be wrong that there was a fresh scepticism about any forecasts for 1990. The need for decisions seemed less urgent. The harsh reality of the depth of failure of the British economy as a whole in 1974–82, along with uncertainty about the effects of revenues from North Sea oil, led to a weakening of interest in the questions about planning the environment of the future.

Permanent dwellings started: by type of authority and sector								
				thousands				
United Kingdom	1971	1976	1977	1978	1979	1980	1981	1982
Public sector								
Local authorities	122.1	133.7	96.8	79.5	58.4	37.5	26.1	35.9
New towns	10.4	14.9	10.6	9.6	8.4	6.8	1.9	2.3
Housing associations	11.2	29.2	28.4	20.9	16.1	15.0	11.9	17.9
Government departments	2.7	2.4	1.1	0.9	0.6	0.1	0.3	0.1
Total	146.4	180.1	136.9	110.9	83.5	59.4	40.3	56.2
Private sector	212.2	158.4	138.6	161.6	148.1	101.4	118.9	145.2
Total dwellings started	358.6	338.5	275.5	272.5	231.7	160.8	159.2	201.3

Question

Discuss the changes in new housing during the period 1971–82, as indicated by this table.

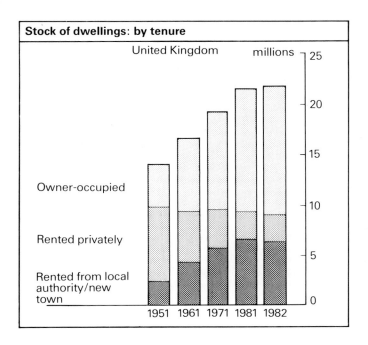

Stock of dwellings: by tenure

United Kingdom — millions

- Owner-occupied
- Rented privately
- Rented from local authority/new town

1951 1961 1971 1981 1982

Question

Discuss the changes in the form of housing tenure indicated by this chart.

Development of forms of transport in Great Britain			
	billions of person-kilometres		
	1961	1971	1982
Private transport	161	330	452
Bus	67	51	40
Train	39	35	31
Air	1	2	3

Question

What are the advantages and disadvantages, for society as a whole, of this increase in travel by private car?

Above: *A modern group practice shared by several G.P.s.*
Below: *A children's ward in a hospital.*

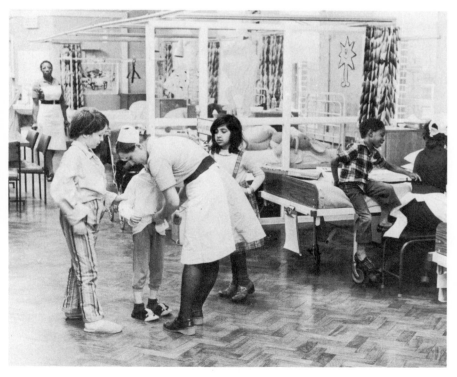

9

The Welfare State

1   Social Security

It is now accepted in Britain that the state should ensure, as far as it
can, than nobody should be without the means of the minimum
necessities of life as the result of unemployment, old age, sickness,
or over-large families. The operations of the welfare state are in
four main parts. First, there is the system of national insurance.
Everybody who is working, either for himself or for an employer,
is obliged to contribute a fixed amount each week to the national
insurance fund, and the fund, which receives supplementary
contributions from the proceeds of general taxation, is used for
paying out benefits to people who are unemployed, or unable to
earn because they are old or sick. Secondly, free or nearly free
medical and dental care is provided for everyone under the
National Health Service, which is financed partly by weekly
contributions paid by people who are working, but mainly by
payments by the state out of general taxation. Thirdly,
supplementary benefits are provided for people whose incomes are
too low for them to be able to live at a minimum standard; the
system of non-contributory payments was extended and refined in
1973–4. Finally, there are many services for the benefit of children,
apart from the provision of education. These benefits include family
allowances, paid to parents in respect of each child, but some
subsidies for children's food have now been restricted to families
who need them.

Every person who is working must make a single national
insurance contribution every week. The amount to be paid each
week is a little more for employees than for people who work on
their own account. In the case of employees, the responsibility for
making the payments belongs to the employer, who must deduct
part of each worker's wage or salary, and add larger sums himself.

But the amount collected in contributions has regularly been little more than half of the total paid out in benefits based on contributions. Payments to retired people are much the biggest item. The deficit is paid for out of general taxation, along with the cost of the National Health Service. This alone is about equal to the total collected in insurance contributions, which in the national accounts tend to be regarded as though they were one source of revenue, akin to ordinary taxation.

The retirement pension, or 'old-age pension' as it is popularly called, may be received by any man from the age of sixty-five (provided he has made his weekly contributions to the fund) if he ceases to work, and by any woman from the age of sixty. A man may continue to work full-time after he is sixty-five, and in that case he gets no pension at first, but when he is over seventy he gets a bigger pension whether he works or not. If he has some small earnings from part-time work, his pension is reduced, but the reduction is less than the amount of his earnings. The normal rate of pension is regularly increased with inflation, but is rather low in comparison with some other European countries. There is also a scheme under which some people may, by paying higher contributions while they are working, receive additional pensions when they retire according to the principle that the state pension, and the contributions towards it, should be related to the amount which a person earned before he retired from his work.

There are in addition non-state methods of providing for retirement pensions. Any person can take a life-insurance policy with an insurance company, and the policy can be devised so as to suit his needs, usually giving him a fixed sum of money at the age of sixty. Most salaried or middle-class type jobs have some system of 'superannuation', with the employer and the employee making payments into a pension fund, and this system is spreading rapidly for some kinds of manual workers too. Many people have one or both of these forms of insurance in addition to the state pension.

If a person becomes unemployed or unable to work because of sickness, he receives payments from the insurance fund at the same rate as the retirement pensioners. The amount of time for which a person is entitled to receive these benefits depends, to some extent, on the length of time for which he has already been paying contributions into the insurance fund. A man may be entitled to unemployment benefit for a period of between five and nineteen months. Sickness benefit is paid for up to 28 weeks, at the same rate as a retirement pension; and after 28 weeks it is replaced by invalidity benefit, at a lower rate—together with supplements if necessary. However, a person in a middle-class salaried job may well be paid his full salary for long periods of absence through sickness. The detailed provisions for state benefits to people who have long illnesses affect mainly manual workers. Employers tend to treat their salaried employees more favourably than their weekly-paid manual workers; the welfare state goes a little of the way towards redressing this difference.

Family allowances are paid directly out of public money contributed by taxpayers, and have nothing to do with the national insurance scheme, though naturally people regard them as part of the ordinary working of the welfare state. An allowance is made for all children in a family. The payments, which are made at post offices, continue until a child leaves school and are subject to income tax. There are special payments for single parent families.

As a final safeguard against poverty, people who prove to the proper authorities that they have not enough to live on may receive Supplementary Benefits (a device that has replaced the older National Assistance). Payments of this type may be used to supplement insurance payments if necessary, and they may include the payment of all or part of the rent of a house or flat. They often affect large families, single women with children, and some old people, and they may supplement the earnings of people who are working but have small earnings, who may also be excused the payment of some or all their local taxes (i.e. 'rates'). Young people who cannot find work after leaving school have to be provided for under these arrangements, and students may draw benefits in their long vacations.

For some people whose skills enable them to find only the lowest-paid jobs, the benefits that they can receive when unemployed may be more than they can earn by working. This is partly because the level of purchasing power considered to be a minimum has been increased, partly because benefits have been raised with inflation more effectively than some earnings; and a big proportion of the people with the lowest earnings are 'self-employed'. Various devices have been developed in attempts to solve this problem—but not with complete success.

After 1979 increased unemployment was a major factor in the increase in the cost of benefits, but the revenue from North Sea oil helped to make it possible to maintain their real level. Although the benefits were less, in terms of real purchasing power, than equivalent benefits in North America or other parts of northern Europe, the level of production was too low to provide adequately for the benefits. This was the main obstacle to the reduction of the retirement age below 65. Recent research found that there were many old people, and some not so old, living in poverty because they did not receive the benefits to which they were entitled. This was because they did not understand the system, or did not know how to apply, or were too proud or too lacking in self-confidence to do anything about it. Great efforts are being made to ensure that such people are helped.

The number of old people is constantly increasing, and although there is much talk and a good deal of action with respect to their special needs, much more still needs to be done. For those who are able to look after themselves, the local authorities have built one-storey houses, often with appropriate surroundings; and the local authorities' health and welfare services can be used by those who need help in their daily lives. There are also residential homes for old people.

Certain types of unpaid service are performed voluntarily by public-spirited people in conjunction with state services. An example is 'meals on wheels'; meals are prepared by the public authorities in a central kitchen and then distributed to infirm old people by women who belong to voluntary organisations, using their own cars.

2   The Health Service

The National Health Service provides free medical treatment both in hospital and outside. It covers sickness of mind as well as ordinary sickness, and it includes the treatment of teeth and the provision of aids to sight and hearing, as well as wheelchairs, artificial limbs and some other expensive items. It was based at first on Acts of Parliament, one for England and Wales passed in 1946 and one for Scotland passed in 1947, but it is possible to talk of a health service covering the whole of Britain, and this discussion covers Scotland as well as England.

People are not obliged to use the service; they may still go to doctors as private patients if they wish to do so, and in big towns there are some private and financially independent hospitals (called 'nursing homes') which people may use rather than the hospitals

A modern old people's home in a new town.

which are within the Health Service. Some people who have
enough money still prefer to be private patients, either because they
do not like to join the common herd, or because they think that
they can in that way establish a more personal relationship with the
doctor, or because, if they are seriously ill or need an operation,
they want to choose for themselves which specialist or surgeon will
treat them without delay.

The idea of the family doctor has always been strong in Britain, and remains so. In order to obtain the benefits of the National Health Service a person must normally be registered on a general practitioner's list, and if he needs medical attention he first goes to his general practitioner or has the general practitioner come to see him. The family doctor gives treatment or prescribes medicine, or, if necessary, arranges for the patient to go to hospital or to be seen at home by a specialist. If the doctor prescribes medicine or pills, his written prescription must be taken to a chemist's shop, where the chemist prepares what is necessary. At first, from 1948, the patient had nothing to pay for medicine, but in 1951 a small fixed payment became necessary. The payment was abolished for a time by the Labour Government in 1964, but then restored by it in 1968. The Health Service funds pay for the cost of each 'prescription' (bottle of medicine or pills) above the patient's contribution, but for small children and people with low incomes there is no charge at all; the health service pays it all.

Each person is free to choose a general practitioner in the area where he lives, and be registered on his list. He must normally go only to the doctor with whom he is actually registered, or to one of the doctor's partners. It is possible to arrange to be transferred to another doctor's list. A person away from home may go to any doctor. Every general practitioner receives a fixed 'capitation' payment from the Health Service funds for each patient on his list. He may also take private patients and earn fees privately for doing various jobs, such as examining people who want to insure their lives with insurance companies. There are about 25,000 general practitioners in the National Health Service and 1,000 outside it. The average doctor thus has a little over 2,000 people on his list; the maximum is around 3,500. Out of his earnings he must usually provide a waiting room and consulting room for his patients, a car and a secretary.

In many towns the health authorities have built Health Centres, in which five or ten or more general practitioners work along with dentists, chiropodists and nurses, often with some shared reception staff and administrative arrangements. On a typical working day a G.P. sees about forty patients, in his surgery, some in the morning, some in the evening; and he spends the afternoon visiting about ten homes of patients whose families have reported that they are too ill to go out. With about six to eight hundred families on his books, the G.P. knows most of them, their personalities, homes and living conditions, their general state of health. He also knows, from his memory and his files, how often and for what reasons he has given each patient a certificate of unfitness for work.

Free birth control advice is normally available at Health Centres, and free abortion may be provided in certain circumstances defined by law.

If a general practitioner or dentist thinks a patient needs to be treated at a hospital (even for an X-ray or blood test) he arranges for him to go to one, sending up the medical records. If necessary the patient is collected in an ambulance, which with its driver and nurse is part of the National Health Service and provided free of charge. Ambulances also collect victims of accidents and other emergencies, and normally these are the only people whom a hospital will receive for treatment without having been referred to it by a general practitioner.

In hospital all treatment, including drugs, is entirely free, both for patients who stay inside and for those who are treated as 'out-patients' and then sent home—by ambulance if necessary, though most patients who can walk are taken home in family cars.

The treatment of teeth has its own separate equivalent of the general practitioner service. Dentists similarly work alone or in partnerships, a few of them in Health Centres; and they too may refer patients to hospital if necessary. At first all dental treatment was provided free of charge, but quite early in the Health Service's history it was decided that patients should pay part of the cost of treatment and for false teeth—except for those aged under twenty-one, nursing and expectant mothers and those too poor to pay.

Eye-testing may be arranged in opticians' shops, where qualified people recommend appropriate glasses. Some of these are doctors, some not. The testing is paid for out of Health Service funds, but most people who need glasses buy them, paying most of the real cost of their provision. Special eye hospitals and dental hospitals treat people who are referred to them, free of charge, and eye hospitals have their own casualty departments for people who come in with injured eyes.

The structure of the National Health Service resembles that of a nationalised industry. Scotland and Wales have their own systems, similar to England's. In England the Secretary of State has general responsibility to Parliament, with a Minister of State for Health under him. He appoints the chairman of the 14 Regional Health Authorities, each based on a university medical school. A typical

Region is divided into about ten to fifteen districts, each based on a big hospital but also covering other hospitals. For each District there is an Authority, with a chairman and about 15 to 20 members, who represent the local government councils and different categories of doctors, nurses, etc. Though not directly elected by the public, the Authorities thus include a big proportion of members whose appointment is essentially political.

In recent years there has been a growth of devices for public participation in matters concerning the management of the Health Service, through elected Community Health Councils and even, at a very local level, informal patients' participation groups. For some kinds of individual complaints, people who feel aggrieved about the working of some aspect of the service may complain to the Health Service Commissioner. This ombudsman receives around 700 complaints a year, and has lately found failures in service or maladministration leading to injustice in about one eighth of the cases brought.

Advances in the technology of medical and surgical treatment have brought great changes to the hospitals, along with a huge increase in their costs. Many old hospitals have been closed, and although new ones have been built, the total number of hospital beds has been reduced. Patients are discharged more quickly than before, after treatment which has become more intensive.

In the mid-1970s the conditions of work of nurses were greatly improved, and by 1983 there were over 100,000 more nurses than in 1970. Meanwhile the number of doctors working in hospitals rose by half, that of technicians even more quickly. The total Health Service staff, including cooks and cleaners, rose to a million. Only the family doctors did not grow in numbers, staying below 30,000. The growing sophistication of treatment and equipment has much to do with this development.

Unlike G.P.s, hospital doctors have salaries with pension rights, a structured career with grades and prospects of promotion. A senior consultant presides over a big empire, particularly if he is in a hospital associated with a university medical school. He may, if he so wishes, work less than full-time, and earn big fees for private work outside. In some places consultants may put their own patients in 'pay beds' in N.H.S. hospitals. However such beds were only one per cent of the total in 1976. The system was attacked by the Labour government, and the number was halved by 1980. Under the Conservatives it then rose again, but very slightly.

The numbers of people choosing to pay for private medical insurance, so that they may have private treatment rather than the N.H.S. treatment for which they have already paid through their taxes, may give some indication of one section of opinion on the N.H.S. The number of people privately insured rose from two per cent of the population in 1961, to four per cent in 1971, to eight per cent in 1982. The total cost of all private treatment was then about one tenth as much as that of the National Health Service.

The cost of the Health Service has risen steadily, so that by the early 1980s its share of the gross national product had risen to about six per cent. In 1983–4 the Thatcher government asked for economies, including a one per cent cut in staff, particularly in the administration. Health Authorities were also required to invite tenders for the separate provision of laundry, catering and cleaning, and to employ the cheapest, whether a private contractor or the existing staff. These measures led to accusations that the government was ruining the Health Service.

In general there is overwhelming evidence suggesting that the vast majority of the public have more respect for the Health Service than for almost any other aspect of state-financed activity. Measurable improvements in the nation's health have not reached Scandinavian levels but in most respects compare well with other European countries. As the total British expenditure on health care absorbs a significantly smaller proportion of the gross national product than in any other Western country, it appears to give the people good value.

3   The Social Services

The aspect of the welfare state which has increased more than any other is in the personal social services. The number of local authority professional social workers of all kinds has multiplied enormously, in line with an unlimited increase in public expectations. Where, up to the 1940s, people as individuals were left to sort out their problems, often helped by idealistic voluntary organisations, now the local authorities' staffs must take responsibility.

Inevitably, for example, some children are ill-treated or neglected at home, or suffer misery or disadvantage as a result of conditions in their homes. Social service staffs have the duty to discover cases of this nature and decide what should be done in an attempt to find a

Prince Charles at the opening of a hostel for young girls.

remedy. If they find that their attempts at help and persuasion do not produce results which they consider satisfactory, and if they see no reason for optimism about the future, they may obtain an order of a court under which a child is put into the care of the local authority. In that case they must decide whether to find a 'foster-home', where a suitable family is prepared to look after the child, or to put the child in one of the authority's own establishments where children are looked after by qualified staff. The Social service workers are also concerned with children who have been found, in the special childrens' courts, to have stolen or committed anti-social acts.

A long established private organisation, financed by subscription, the National Society for the Prevention of Cruelty to Children, is still active, and works with the local authority social services staff. But the number of professional social workers has increased enormously, along with their load of work. Authoritarian approaches are avoided.

Work with children is only a part of the social workers' task. The local authorities have duties which extend to a concern with all kinds of deprivation or maladjustment; the welfare state works not only through social security payments and the Health Service, but also through active involvement in positive attempts to promote welfare in cases where neither money payments nor medical treatment can suffice. Just as the demands on the Health Service have grown, so too have the demands on this other aspect of the social services; and the fastest growth was before the sharp rise in unemployment after 1976.

Health expenditure: 1982		
	expenditure per inhabitant	per cent of G.N.P.
	£ sterling equivalent	
Britain	258	5.3
West Germany	595	8.8
France	503	8.1
Netherlands	529	8.7
Denmark	492	7.5
Sweden	598	9.6
Switzerland	670	6.8
U.S.A.	823	9.9

Question

Britain spends less on health care than other industrialised countries – do you think this is reflected in the scope of care provided?

National Health Service - annual costs per person[*]: by age and sex, 1981		
Great Britain	£s per person	
	males	females
Age		
Under 1	473	386
1- 4	178	157
5-15	111	100
16-24	114	111
25-44	126	131
45-64	193	184
65-74	407	370
75 or over	772	947
All ages	192	222

*Excludes maternity (obstetrics, in-patients and out-patients, and midwifery), administration, and capital costs

Question

What does this table suggest for future health expenditure as the number of elderly people increases?

Above: Children at primary school.
Below: Winchester, one of Britain's most famous public schools for boys.

10

Schools and Universities

1   The Educational System

Education is compulsory for all children aged 5 to 16 years. Nine-tenths of all children are educated in 'state schools' (actually run by the local education authorities). The division between primary and secondary education is at the age of eleven, when almost all children in the state system change schools. At the age of sixteen about two-thirds of these pupils leave school and get jobs or apprenticeships (if they can). A large proportion take part-time (or full-time) courses, mainly related to work-skills, in the technical and commercial colleges which are also operated by local authorities. About one-third stay on at school until the age of eighteen, preparing themselves for advanced level examinations.

The state system has effectively taken over and incorporated most of the schools originally founded by churches. Complex laws define the right of a church to keep some power, including influence over appointment of some teachers, in a school to whose costs it makes a small contribution. About one-quarter of children aged under eleven are in Church of England schools, but there are few Church of England secondary schools. There is, on the other hand, a whole range of Catholic primary and secondary schools, including some newly-built. The whole of this system of education is provided free of charge to pupils, paid for by the public's taxes. It absorbs more than 6% of the gross national product.

Some parents prefer not to use the 'state' system but pay for their children to be educated at independent schools. These account for less than one-tenth of all children, but this private sector includes the so-called 'public schools', some of whose names are known all over the world, and whose importance is out of proportion to their numbers. They will be discussed separately in this chapter.

Preparation for examinations is not the first purpose of

education, but before we go on to look at the various types of schools in detail it may be useful to mention the main certificates which indicate educational attainments. Moderately assiduous children take the Certificate of Secondary Education (C.S.E.) which indicates satisfactory completion of schooling to sixteen. More ambitious children take the examinations for the General Certificate of Education (G.C.E.) at ordinary level. This may be taken in any number of subjects, and some children take as many as ten subjects. Many, after gaining this certificate, leave school to start training for various careers; the certificate is the required starting-point for many types of professional training.

Most young people who stay at school after passing their ordinary level examinations prepare themselves for an attempt to win a certificate at advanced level, usually in only two or three subjects. During the last years at school the pupils are almost obliged to specialise in narrow fields, as the advanced level certificate demands intensive study of the two or three subjects in which the examination is taken. Some people believe that English education at this level is too highly specialised. In Scotland it is much broader and the Scottish Higher Certificate may well cover five subjects.

The examinations for the General Certificate of Education are not conducted by the state or by any public authority, but by various examining boards, each of which arranges its syllabus, prepares question-papers, grades the candidates and awards certificates. In England there are six of these examining boards, each connected with a university or a group of universities, and certain other boards as well. The examinations set by the different boards differ in content and arrangement, but not in difficulty. In practice each school prepares its pupils for the examinations of one of the boards.

A student who receives further full-time education after the age of eighteen, either at a university or at some other college giving training of a special type, can usually receive a grant from the public authorities to cover his expenses, or almost all of them, unless his parents have a large income. But the number of young people who can enter universities is limited by the capacity of the universities, which is less than enough to take all the young people who have the basic qualifications, in the form of general certificates at advanced level, for university admission. In practice, therefore, entry to the universities is competitive. But university degree courses are also available at polytechnics, and entry to the Open University is less restricted.

In the teaching profession there is no clear distinction between elementary and advanced-level school-teachers. Fixed supplements are paid to teachers who have first or second class honours degrees from their universities, and various supplements to teachers who have posts of special responsibility and to some teachers in schools which have children in advanced-level classes. Schools outside the state system make their own arrangements for paying their teachers.

All discussion of English education is complicated by confusion in the terminology. Acts of Parliament use terms with precise meaning, but many of these terms are very cumbersome and avoided in ordinary conversation. There are not even any standard names or numbers for the grades or age-levels in schools, though inside a particular school it is usual to count upwards, with the lowest class called the first. A class is often called a 'form', never a 'grade'. There is a convention, not universally followed, that the top class should be called the Sixth, and when teachers talk about the 'Sixth Form' they almost always mean the top-level class of a higher secondary school, doing advanced work beyond the ordinary level G.C.E.

The academic year begins after the summer holidays and is divided into three 'terms', with the intervals between them formed by the Christmas and Easter holidays. The exact dates of the holiday vary from area to area, being in general about two weeks at Christmas and Easter, plus often a week or more at Whitsun, and six weeks in the summer, beginning rather late. Schools outside the state system decide on their own holiday dates, generally taking a month off at Christmas and Easter and eight weeks in the summer. The three terms are not everywhere called by the same names; some schools call the January-March period 'the Spring Term', others call it 'Easter Term', 'Hilary Term' or 'Epiphany Term'. All this illustrates a very English individualism, harmless enough but confusing and often rather pointless.

Day-schools mostly work Mondays to Fridays only, from about 9 a.m. to between 3 and 4 p.m. Lunch is provided and parents pay part of the cost unless, by a complicated formula, they show that their income is low enough to entitle them to free children's meals. Out of 9 million children of all ages in maintained schools in 1977, $5\frac{1}{2}$ million took school meals, 14% of them without payment; the rest brought their own sandwiches or went home for lunch. The total tax-subsidy to school meals came to nearly £400 million, or 7% of the cost of education. To put it in another way, this worked out on average at 40 pence per lunch per day, or £80 per child per year.

2   State Education

State education is in two main stages: primary up to the age of eleven, and secondary from eleven to eighteen. The primary stage is subdivided, with the period between five and seven years being generally called 'infants'.

Nearly all children change schools at the age of eleven, even if they have to travel a long way to the secondary school. Boys and girls are together in nearly all primary schools, and at the secondary level only a few separate schools for boys or girls still survive. The changeover to co-educational secondary education has been accepted with virtually no opposition.

Everywhere in England the education committee of the local elected council is responsible for all the schools, except for those which are 'independent' and a few which receive direct grants from the state and form a special category.

The 'state' schools in inner London are run by the Inner London Education Authority, in outer London by the London boroughs, in metropolitan counties by the districts. In all of the rest of England the schools are under the control of the county councils. The education committee of a council which has charge of schools is known as the Local Education Authority.

State laws provide a general framework within which the schools operate and the central government provides a large part of the money, but there is only a fairly loose state control over the schools throughout the country. The Department of Education and Science establishes standards to which schools ought to conform and it sends out Her Majesty's Inspectors, who are officials of the Department, to visit and make thorough reports on the work of every school from time to time. They give advice to the teachers and suggest new ideas, but their function is above all advisory. In every school the head teacher has a great deal of autonomy in deciding what is to be taught and how the teaching is to be carried out.

Most primary schools are wholly owned and controlled (technically *maintained*) by the local authorities, but about one-third belong to churches, either Anglican or Roman Catholic, having been founded by religious bodies with the idea of providing not only general education but also religious instruction according to the ideas of particular denominations. When education became universal and free these church schools were taken into the general system but kept some degree of independence. The general principle is that the more money the church contributes towards the cost of maintaining the buildings the more independence it keeps, the more positions on the board of managers, the more control over the appointment of teachers.

In the schools not connected with churches, religion is not neglected. In all schools run by local authorities the day must, by law, begin with prayers, and there is religious instruction, though both the prayers and the religious teaching are supposed to be 'Christian' without leaning towards any particular type of Christianity.

In primary schools the boys and girls are very often—but not always—kept together. With the children beginning to go to school at the age of five it is possible to make an early start with learning to read, though they spend much of their time at first in doing things which could not properly be called 'work'. There has been much development in recent times of imaginative ideas in educational methods, and in particular much progress has been made, even in schools which are in old buildings, with the improvement of the decoration and furnishing of classrooms. Some people complain that there is not enough hard learning in the schools. There is indeed evidence that standards of attainment have fallen, and in 1976 the Prime Minister, Mr Callaghan, initiated a great debate about the best way of curing the deficiencies.

For all children in state schools, secondary education begins at the age of eleven. Each local education authority is obliged by the 1944 Education Act to provide secondary schools of sufficient variety to cater for the abilities and aptitudes of children in its area. Until about 1965 most local authorities provided two main types of secondary school:'grammar schools' giving a liberal and scientific education up to the age of eighteen, preparing pupils for the General Certificate of Education and in some cases for university entrance; and 'secondary modern schools', which give general education, including some practical instruction, up to the age of fifteen.

By about 1960 the division of children between the two types of secondary school was widely unpopular, particularly among people who were politically on the left. It looked like the beginning of a separation into classes that would continue throughout life—and the proportion of manual workers' children who went to grammar schools was low. Also, provision of grammar school places varied from area to area, from 15% to 40%.

A few comprehensive secondary schools, with children not separated according to ability, were established before 1960. Since then most local authorities have gone over completely to the comprehensive system; others are changing slowly. Lately, all newly built secondary schools have been comprehensive; some old grammar or secondary schools have been converted. By 1977, 90 per cent of all state school pupils aged 11 to 16 were in comprehensive schools, and very few in the surviving selective 'grammar schools'. The Labour government of 1966–70 pressed the local authorities to move fast towards making the comprehensive system universal, and after 1974 attempted some coercion. The Conservatives argued that each local authority should make its own plans without pressure from the central government—though it too required specific projects to be submitted to the Secretary of State for Education for approval.

As the comprehensive secondary schools replaced the separate grammar and secondary modern schools in the 1960s and 70s, it was accepted that a true comprehensive needed to include a 'sixth form', or classes for pupils aged 16 to 18. But a 'sixth form' with less than 100 pupils in each year cannot provide teaching in minority subjects, such as Spanish, unless it makes uneconomical use of its teachers through very small classes. The first solution to this problem was by making comprehensives very big, often with 300 pupils in each year from 11 to 16, and sometimes by incorporating two or three formerly separate schools into a single school, pending the building of a new one. Another solution, more used in the 1970s, is to move sixteen year-olds to sixth form colleges, or to make divisions at other ages.

Every school has a name, normally including the description of its type. It is gradually becoming common to use the title 'High School' for a comprehensive, following American practice. Until recently that description was used almost exclusively for girls' secondary schools in the private sector.

A secondary school maintained by a local authority, whether secondary modern, grammar or comprehensive, is one among thirty or fifty or a hundred schools under the same local direction.

The head teacher (usually a man unless the school is for girls only) has a good deal of freedom to design the teaching together with his staff, and schools are not all the same in curriculum or atmosphere. But there are some characteristics to be found in nearly all English secondary schools, reflecting the influence of the independent 'public' schools and nowadays subject to some questioning.

Secondary schools of all types try seriously to build up the sense that the school is a real community, with its hierarchy of order and authority. Every school wants a hall, big enough to accommodate all the pupils, and this is expensive to build. The morning begins with Assembly, for prayers and announcements. An educational sociologist, Ronald King, who has studied the process in a sample of 72 schools, describes his findings:

'Pupils enter the school hall supervised by the prefects (12 per cent) or the teachers (82 per cent). They enter by age group (60 per cent) and take up special positions for each age group (88 per cent). The head teacher enters separately from all others (83 per cent), and takes up his position on the platform (92 per cent) behind a lectern (65 per cent) . . .

Most head teachers saw the school as a community, and nearly two thirds of them saw the assembly as fostering this idea.'
(Ronald King. 'School Rituals.' *New Society* July 1973, pp. 71ff.)

The curriculum for children aged 11 to 16 gives them scope for choice, and the Certificate of Secondary Education enables children to be examined in skills which are not strictly academic, as well as in the normal academic school subjects. The teaching day is typically divided into seven periods of forty minutes each, and these include periods for football, hockey and other sports on the playing fields beside the school buildings, as well as for Physical Education in the gymnasium.

The old practice of streaming, or teaching children in classes separated according to ability, has become unfashionable. Mixed-ability classes are obviously less 'élitist' than streamed ones, and some inconclusive evidence suggests that children of high ability do not develop more quickly when they are separated from the rest. This argument is not settled; it has political implications.

For two or three decades there has been a deliberate intention to slant the teaching towards understanding rather than mere learning. History is heavily slanted towards aspects appropriate to children's age; nothing must be inert. Geography is not just learning location and products. Rather than learn mathematical procedures, children are supposed to learn the essential relations between figures. However, a survey, published in 1978, of the mathematical skills of children of various ages showed an incredibly large proportion to be incapable of doing the elementary sums needed for understanding the world or even for the ordinary processes of shopping. Ability to read and write English adequately is not widespread, and adequate knowledge of any foreign language restricted to a few. Some observers criticise modern education for failing to instil the discipline of learning, some go further and claim that children learn that they have a right to what they want or think they want, and a right not to do things they do not like. Others reject such 'reactionary' and unfashionable views; but the demand for better standards of attainment, inspired by Mr Callaghan in 1976, may tilt the balance a little in the 1980s.

Advanced level work in the sixth form (that is, at the top of the school) tends to be rather highly specialised, so that a boy or girl studies only a few subjects. Latin and Greek are rapidly losing popularity, particularly now that universities no longer demand one of them as an entrance requirement. History, French and English are very popular subjects, and many schools now provide teaching in Economics. Everyone wants to see more scientific education, but so many newly-trained scientists go into industry that the schools are finding it difficult to expand their scientific teaching. Even among boys, specialists in the Sciences are increasing at a slower rate than are specialists in the Arts.

Local authorities also provide technical and commercial colleges, which are remarkably active and many-sided institutions, whose work is developing very rapidly. They are for the most part not like ordinary schools, in that most of their pupils, or rather their students, are not undergoing full-time courses of instruction. A large part of their work consists in the provision of evening courses for people who have left school and are working in ordinary jobs during the daytime, together with some courses during the day, mainly for young people who have jobs but who are released from their jobs for one or two days each week. Their main function is to provide courses in technical and commercial subjects leading to many kinds of certificates and diplomas, but they also prepare students for the General Certificate of Education or for some other certificates of similar type and status. Thus if a boy has left school without taking this examination, it is usually possible for him to study for it at a technical college after leaving school. Many of these colleges also provide courses which people attend on one or two evenings a week, not for the purpose of obtaining any professional qualification, but in order to improve their knowledge in some field or other as an end in itself. They embody the principle that education does not end when a child leaves school, and are centres of quite an active social and cultural life in their communities.

Although the technical colleges are doing so much in the field of education for adolescents and adults, there are still other types of adult education which are flourishing in a different way. The Workers' Educational Association is a voluntary organisation, which now works in collaboration with university extra-mural boards which get funds, ultimately, from the state. Their main function is the provision of weekly meetings of classes for adults, during the winter months, for discussion of subjects of the type which are studied in universities, but without leading to diplomas or certificates.

3 Independent Schools

About 8% of children aged 11 to 16 were, in 1984, in independent schools outside the state system. These are of many different types. Most of their pupils are sent to them because their parents wish to exercise choice and are willing and able to pay fees. A small proportion of pupils are paid for by local authorities for various reasons. These reasons may include the absence of a state school with facilities suitable for a child or for its parents' requirements. In 1978 a government circular told local authorities not to pay fees for independent education on the ground of children's academic merit.

The so-called 'public schools' form a small part of private-sector education. They are (mainly) boarding schools for 500 to 800 boys or girls between the ages of 13 and 18—though some of them take some day-pupils too, and the proportion of day-pupils is increasing. A few of the boys' schools began in the 1970s to take a few girls over 16 too, for 'sixth form' work in preparation for the advanced level General Certificate of Education.

The term 'public school' is obviously misleading, because the schools are in fact private. There is no agreed definition of the term. Up to about 1950 about 80 boys' boarding schools, together with a few London day-schools, were commonly regarded as 'public schools'. Since then the term has been extended to cover about 120 other schools, mostly with few or no boarding pupils. Most of this second group cover the full range of secondary education (11 to 18) and had until 1975 a special status as 'direct grant schools' in relation to the state system.

The Headmasters' Conference is a vigorous organisation whose members are the heads of boys' schools which fulfil certain criteria, including proportions of boys in the 'sixth form' and continuing to university; but it is in fact misleading to equate public schools with membership of this body, which includes the whole group of 200 schools in the broader definition, as well as some others.

The group of about 80 boys' public schools, narrowly defined, educates only about 2% of all English boys (less than this in Wales and Scotland), but deserves special attention. These public schools have been, since 1800, England's most peculiar and characteristic contribution to educational practice, and they have had some influence on secondary education as a whole. Almost all were founded before the state began to involve itself in education. Some were founded in the middle ages, some around 1600, some after 1840, a few after 1920.

Until the 1970s most of the people in leading positions in society sent their sons to boarding schools, and most people who attained such positions were former public school pupils. Even in 1984 they include three-quarters of Conservative M.P.s, most of the bishops, generals in the army, high court judges, directors of banks and insurance companies, and a big proportion of people in leading positions in other professions. With their small classes, high academic standards, good facilities for sport, music and the arts, they provide good education. They can attract good and dedicated teachers. With their relatively high general level of sophistication their pupils give some inspiration to each other.

They have their place in literature. Several best-selling books, particularly of the period from 1900 to 1930, are based on life in imaginary public schools; so too were some widely read boys' magazines of that period and after. Until about the 1950s these schools had many nasty qualities, with irrational rules and discipline that oppressed younger boys—enforced mainly by older boys whom the masters appointed to positions of authority as prefects (or 'monitors' or 'praeposters'—each school has its own private language). Since the 1960s the harsh discipline has been abated; in this and other matters the schools have shown belated skill in adapting themselves to new values, in which humanitarianism is predominant. They are no longer barbarous, but their buildings are old and uncomfortable.

Their fees are high: about £5,000 a year in 1984, plus a few hundred pounds for travel and other incidental costs. To send two children to a public school would absorb the whole of a senior teacher's take-home earnings. Yet the schools were still full in 1984, with pupils' fees paid out of capital or by grandparents, or through long-term insurance policies. The schools themselves receive a small proportion of pupils at reduced fees, or even (in very few cases) free of charge—but attendance at a public school is in practice reserved almost exclusively for the children of the relatively rich, including now more and more from other countries.

It is usually fairly easy to distinguish a man over 40 who was educated at a public school from other men. Because of all this the public schools have come to be associated in many people's minds with hereditary privilege. They have had a profound effect in raising and maintaining the consciousness of class divisions, and for several generations England was dominated by public school men. If it were not for the public schools, the sense of class would not have developed as it has.

The Labour Party is very hostile to what it sees as a major source of socio-economic privilege. It has hoped to kill the system by providing adequate education free of charge, but the unhappy reputation of the comprehensive schools has in the 1980s had the opposite effect.

One curious reaction of the Labour government in 1975 affected, not the 80 public schools narrowly interpreted, but many of the (approximately) 120 other boys' day schools of the Headmasters' Conference. These in their turn have educated a further 3% of the population, chosen mainly on grounds of academic merit.

In most towns the principal grammar schools, established before the intervention of the state, were until 1975 enabled to stay out of the control of local councils, but to receive each a direct grant from the state, while remaining independent. In these direct grant schools, before 1975, about half to three-quarters of the pupils paid no fees; the others paid but at less than the true economic cost (typically, £200 a year in 1974). The pupils were chosen by competitive tests at the age of eleven. By 1974 some of these schools had an academic reputation equal to that of the most prestigious public schools, and, as members of the Headmasters' Conference, were often described as 'public schools'.

In 1975 the Labour government, in an attempt to combat

privilege, abolished the 'direct grant' status. The schools' governing bodies had to make a choice: either to abandon their independence and hand the school over to the local authority, or to continue as independent schools, supported by parents' fees. Most remained independent, and by 1984 their fees were around £1,500 a year.

Until now the discussion has been restricted to boys' schools. Education for girls has followed a similar pattern, but with less social and political significance. Since the late nineteenth century there have also been corresponding girls' schools in a similar pattern; and after 1900 a few essentially similar schools for boys and girls together. These have included independent schools (often called 'public schools') and others with direct grant status, which was abolished in 1975.

For primary education, up to the age of thirteen, 'preparatory' schools for boys are a usual preliminary to admission to the inner group of about 80 'public schools' (narrowly conceived). Some of these are attached to public schools; others, mainly with less than 100 pupils, are separate private institutions, now usually with governing bodies like those of the public schools.

By 1978 the independent schools had dropped their old sense of deliberate superiority. Their pupils were following popular values, behaviour and dress, rather than leading. Popular magazines about public school life had disappeared—though writers of the older generation concerned themselves extensively with the public schools of the past, including their brutality. The old sense of snobbery which once sustained the social differences associated with private education was by this time almost entirely dead. Churchill's three successors as Conservative Party Leaders (Eden, Macmillan and Douglas-Home) had all been educated at the same public school (Eton); indeed Douglas-Home was the 18th Old Etonian among the 36 men who were prime ministers in a period of 200 years. But Heath and Mrs Thatcher did not conform to that pattern; even within the Conservative Party an education at Eton would now probably be a handicap to an ambitious politician.

Modern Conservatives are embarrassed by the èlitism of their past; yet they do accept differentiation based on quality of work, and admire the academic standards which the independent schools are still maintaining, perhaps with more vigour than they did in previous generations. The public schools were still alive in 1978, whether seen narrowly or broadly. Their reduced emphasis on sport had given them more scope for developing the more varied aspects of their pupils' talents. Objectively, they probably had more real merit than fifty years before. But this did not save them from egalitarian resentment.

4 Some Educational Problems

British education has many critics, and much of the criticism has a political basis. The system is supposed to provide equality of opportunity for all, but it is not to be denied that it is sustaining inequality. Probably it is also failing to develop much potential talent and ability. In 1959 a document known as the Crowther Report was published by a committee which the Government had set up. It quoted a survey which showed that, while 28% of all children stayed at school beyond the age of fifteen, only 8% of unskilled workers' children did so; and only 1% of children of unskilled workers' received full-time education beyond the age of eighteen, in comparison with 34% of children of people in the professional and managerial class. This situation was generally regarded as unsatisfactory, but other countries in Europe—even in Communist Eastern Europe—have found themselves faced by a similar problem.

Three approaches have been tried since 1960, promoted with confident enthusiasm by the Left, and on the whole supported, but with scepticism, by the Right, which has at the same time pressed the claims of high academic standards. The gradual elimination of selective secondary education in the state system began about 1960 and by 1978 was almost complete, but the new comprehensive schools are in some difficulty. In order to ensure that a school would have enough pupils continuing beyond the ordinary level at sixteen to ensure a sixth form big enough for a wide variety of subjects, many comprehensive schools have been set up with an annual intake of 250 to 300 eleven year-olds. This makes them very big, with less personal contact. And even so, the average comprehensive school sixth form does not have enough pupils wishing to study Russian or Spanish—or even German—to justify the teaching of these and other minority-interest subjects.

A survey of 1978 indicated that 6% of people then aged 18 to 23 could read a German newspaper (while nearly half of West Germans could manage English); nearly a quarter of the English could read French, and one per cent Spanish. Very few indeed could manage any other language.

In 1972 the school-leaving age was, after some postponement, raised from 15 to 16 years. Attempts at controlling the 10% of fifteen year-olds who resent being obliged to stay at school absorb much of the teachers' efforts, to the detriment of their more co-operative pupils. The Certificate of Secondary Education, less demanding than the ordinary level G.C.E., has been quite popular, and a realistic goal for some; but for others, the values of the gang outside are more attractive and more compelling. Truancy, vandalism and violence have increased, especially in schools in some central areas of cities.

The punishment of school pupils by beating with a stick or strap was still quite widely used up to the early 1980s. After some parents had brought complaints to the European Court of Human Rights, the Court ruled, in 1982, that corporal punishment was degrading and in breach of the Human Rights convention. By 1984 Parliament had discussed the matter but taken no legislative action, but about half of all local education authorities had either finally forbidden the practice in all their schools or reached a stage in the process leading to abolition. It seemed very likely that others would soon follow them.

In an age where the loudest voices claim that all conventional authority is oppressive, the moderately-liberal teacher is not well placed; and the teachers' union's readiness to use militant actions in support of demands for better pay or fringe-benefits has been in conflict with the vestiges of conventional authority attached to the teacher's role. Teachers are not well paid. Yet the degree of success that they have had in pressing their claims has contributed to the rising expenditure on education. By 1978, as a result of the decline in the birthrate from about 1965, the drop in the number of children had begun to move up into the schools.

Government policy reacted slowly to the evidence of the statistics; by 1975 there was a sudden and painful reduction in the number of teachers in training. By 1978 15,000 qualified teachers, wishing to teach, were unemployed. They might well have been employed, with a consequent reduction of the excessive numbers in school classes, if expenditure on education had been increased. But with all public expenditure, whether on social services or any other purpose, already at a daunting level, there was not much prospect of bringing the unemployed teachers into the empty classrooms.

With state education faced by all these problems, there were new incentives for parents to make financial sacrifices to send their children to schools outside the system, and thus to sustain the fundamental inequalities in society which the proponents of equal education wanted to destroy.

5   The Universities

There are more than forty universities in Britain—nearly twice as many as in 1960. During the 1960s eight completely new ones were founded, and ten other new ones were created by converting old colleges of technology into universities. In 1960–78 the number of students increased from 70,000 to 280,000. By 1978 about 12% of men aged eighteen to twenty-one were in universities—and about 8% of women.

All British universities are private institutions. Each has its own governing council, including some local businessmen and local politicians as well as a few academics. The state began to give grants to them sixty years ago. Students have to pay fees and living costs, but every student may receive from the local authority of the place

King's College, Cambridge: one of Britain's oldest university buildings.

Sussex University, one of Britain's more modern universities.

where he lives a personal grant which is enough to pay his full costs, including lodging and food—unless his parents are rich. Most students take jobs in the summer for about six weeks, but they do not normally do outside work during the academic session.

The Government gives money to the universities to cover the cost of buildings and to cover almost the whole of their current expenditure. The Department of Education and Science does not exercise direct control, but it can have important influence on new developments through its power to allocate funds. It takes the advice of the University Grants Committee, a body which is mainly composed of academics.

Each university has its own syllabuses, and there are some quite important differences between one and another. In general the Bachelor's degree is given to students who pass examinations at the end of three or four years of study, Bachelor of Arts for History, Philosophy, Language and Literature and sometimes Social Studies or Theology, or Bachelor of Science or Commerce or Music. Honours degrees are classified according to the candidate's examination performance. Typically about 5% are put in the first class, 30% upper second class, 40% lower second, while the rest are distributed between third class, pass and fail. About 15% of students who start at universities leave without obtaining a degree, some of them after only one year.

The first postgraduate degree is normally that of Master, conferred for a thesis based on at least one year's full-time work; the time actually taken is usually more than a year. Recently there has been an increase in Masters' degrees based mainly on course work and examinations. In most universities it is only in the science faculties that any large numbers of students stay to do postgraduate work. Oxford and Cambridge are peculiar in that they give the Master of Arts degree automatically to any Bachelor who pays the necessary fees at any time after the seventh year from his first admission to the university, and in Scotland the degree of Master of Arts is given as a first degree, being equivalent to an English Bachelor's degree. Everywhere the degree of Doctor of Philosophy is given for a thesis which is an original contribution to knowledge.

Among the English universities Oxford and Cambridge have a special eminence, and they are different from the others. Every other university in England and Wales was founded after 1820, but Oxford's first college claims to have been founded in 1249, Cambridge's first in 1348.

Oxford had seventeen colleges, all for men, by 1600, Cambridge sixteen, and others have been added later, as well as five for women at Oxford and three at Cambridge, beginning in 1869. With about 12,000 students each, the two ancient universities, each in the centre of a town of 100,000 people, are similar in most respects—even including the domination of each by three specially eminent colleges—so a brief description of Oxford covers the main characteristics of Cambridge too.

Oxford University is a federation of parallel colleges, some big, some small, each governed by its staff, collectively called 'Fellows', and each with a chief, entitled Master, Warden, Provost, Rector, Principal, President or Dean. One ancient college (All Souls) has no students; ten others, all fairly new, have only postgraduates. The main part of the university consists of twenty-eight ordinary colleges, each of which has its own dining hall, library and chapel, and enough rooms for about half of its 200 to 400 students, who may study any of the subjects taught in the university. The Fellows teach the students in the small groups of two or three, but send them out to tutors in other colleges for the more specialised subjects, or to the university laboratories for scientific subjects. Lectures are open to all students; some are given in college lecture rooms, others in buildings belonging to the university, which, as a federal body, operates the examinations, provides the central laboratories and arranges lecture-courses. Most of the main college buildings are more than 300 years old, but there are some new blocks of rooms, which are more comfortable but less attractive. Few places in the world are more rewarding to a visitor—except perhaps Cambridge, whose finest buildings are more accessible and less scattered.

Together Oxford and Cambridge universities have now less than one-tenth of all British university students; yet all nine leaders of the Labour, Conservative and Liberal Parties in 1955–75 were educated at Oxford; so too most of the other prominent Labour and Conservative ministers, including (on the Labour side) Jenkins, Healey, Crossman, Crosland, Foot and Benn. Former students of Oxford and Cambridge dominated English politics—as well as the law, banking and the higher Civil Service—no less in 1975 than a hundred or two hundred years before. The élitism which these facts imply was much criticised in the 1970s. The two great universities work hard to justify their position, and the young people who have had success in work or sport compete for places in the colleges; but the established pre-eminence will probably be weakened in the next twenty years.

Oxford's Bodleian Library and the Cambridge University Library are entitled, by long-established law, to receive a free copy of every book published in the United Kingdom. The Ashmolean Museum at Oxford and the Fitzwilliam at Cambridge have some of the most important collections in England outside London. There is no finer church in England than the chapel of King's College, Cambridge; the chapel of one Oxford college (less distinguished architecturally) serves also as the cathedral of the diocese. Of the two, Oxford is the more sceptical; few Oxford men would be ready to define the purposes of their work except in the vaguest terms.

After 1970 a few of the old men's colleges began to accept women students too. This revolution soon spread to others, and by 1979 all but six of the colleges were co-educational; three of the 'conservative' ones were still for men only, three for women. Another revolution has removed all the old restrictions on students' freedom.

England had no other universities, apart from Oxford and Cambridge, until the nineteenth century. Scotland, however, had four, all founded before A.D. 1600. Three of these, Glasgow, Edinburgh and Aberdeen, are in the chief cities, and their students have generally lived at home or found their own lodgings; the fourth, St Andrews, has always had some features in common with Oxford and Cambridge.

The first English university to be founded after Oxford and Cambridge was at Durham, a small cathedral city in the far north. Durham University came into existence in 1832. It has always been based on a college system, partly resembling that of Oxford and Cambridge, but its teaching is arranged as at other provincial universities. The University of London, consisting at first of two colleges, was given a charter in 1836; later many more colleges were added, and there are now about twenty colleges and schools of the university, apart from its medical schools and other professional schools. The teaching is in the colleges, which are placed in various parts of the capital, and most of which are not residential. There are now more than 40,000 students. The constitution of the university is very complicated; its main function is to conduct examinations and grant degrees for the students in the various colleges and for the external students, many of whom are scattered all over Britain, and, indeed, all over the world.

During the nineteenth century, institutions of higher education were founded in most of the biggest industrial towns and in a few other centres. For a long time they could not give degrees themselves, but prepared students for the London University examinations. They were called 'university colleges', because they were not universities in their own right. Their first purpose was to provide higher education for local inhabitants who could not afford the cost of going away from home for their studies. One by one these colleges, as they grew bigger and more solidly established, were given charters and became independent universities. All of them have now achieved independent status, some only since 1945. Now there are established universities in London, Durham, Manchester, Liverpool, Birmingham, Leeds, Sheffield, Bristol, Reading, Nottingham, Leicester, Southampton, Exeter, Hull and Newcastle upon Tyne. In Wales there are four similar institutions, dating from the same period, united rather uncomfortably as the University of Wales.

In 1949 a new university was founded in the grounds of an old country mansion at Keele, Staffordshire. Following this, the early 1960s produced a spate of completely new foundations, each in a campus near a not-too-large, not-too-industrial town; the Universities of York and Lancaster, of Sussex, Kent, Warwick, Essex and East Anglia. Taking the name from the county seems to reflect American ideas. Each of these new universities, like Keele, has its own approach to teaching.

Then in the middle 1960s there was a further new development. Among the five hundred local technical colleges maintained by local authorities a few had already gained special prestige. By 1967 ten of these had been given charters as new universities, though still concentrating mostly on science and technology, with languages and social sciences on a smaller scale. Most of these are in the biggest cities where there are already established universities, and now some cities have two universities each. So now we have the University of Aston (Birmingham), Salford (close to Manchester), Strathclyde (Glasgow), Heriot-Watt University (Edinburgh), Brunel (London) and the City University of London; also universities at Bradford (Yorkshire) and Loughborough (near Nottingham). A few others among these newest foundations are being developed in completely new sites; thus the Bristol College of Technology has become the University of Bath, in completely new buildings 30 kilometres from its original home. Also, the old Battersea Technical College (South London) has become the new University of Surrey, at Guildford, 50 kilometres away.

When we add all these together we find that the number of universities in England increased within ten years from nineteen to thirty-six, and in Scotland from four to eight, including the new University of Stirling and the newly-independent University of Dundee.

All the middle-aged universities were founded, and at first developed, with money provided by private donors, many of whom were local industrialists. In recent years they have received most of their financial needs from the state, but their original constitution and organisation have not been altered. Each has a non-academic Chancellor, who is usually a man prominent in public life, but who is not paid and is not expected to be more than a figurehead. The effective chief is the Vice-Chancellor, who is a professional academic. The highest governing body is usually a council consisting of a few professors together with some local notables; under it is a Senate whose composition is entirely academic, and which receives advice from the boards of the various faculties. The teaching is organised in departments, such as History, French, Geology, etc., though the newest universities are devising new patterns of syllabus.

Each department has its chief, who usually has the title of Professor, unless the department is very small. A big department may have more than one professor. Other teachers do not have the title of professor, but are entitled 'Lecturers', though some senior teachers or heads of small departments have the intermediate title of 'Reader' or 'Senior Lecturer'. About one in six of all university teachers are professors. When a university teaching post is vacant it is usually advertised in newspapers, and the appointment is made by the council on the advice of a small committee of senior teachers, who choose the three or four best-qualified applicants and decide between them on the basis of references and interviews.

Although the large city universities were at first intended to be used mainly by local residents who would live at home, after 1945 all the English universities followed Oxford and Cambridge in becoming national rather than local institutions. At most English universities between 80% and 95% of students are not local residents. About 3,000 young people whose family homes are in Bristol are students at universities, but less than 100 of them are in Bristol University; 97% are at other universities. The students at Bristol University come from all over England, particularly the London area. This is made possible by the automatic payment of grants to cover the cost of studying away from home. In most cases about half to two-thirds of the students live in halls of residence; the older halls provide meals in hall, the newest provide kitchens for the students. Other students now live two or three together in rented flats.

Each university decides each year how many students it proposes to admit to each of its courses, and chooses the right number of applicants on the basis of merit. People who wish to enter a university fill up a long form which they obtain from the Universities Central Council for Admissions, and name up to five universities at which they would like to study particular courses, in their order of preference. For each course at a university, applicants are placed in order of apparent merit—and merit is judged by a combination of examination marks, school teachers' confidential reports and (in some cases) special written and/or oral tests.

No specified grade in the advanced level G.C.E. examinations confers any right to admission to a university. Each student who 'passes' an advanced level examination is awarded a mark of 1 to 5 points, and universities do not normally admit anyone with less than two passes at the lowest grade (2 points). In fact the average advanced level score of all students admitted in 1977 was $9\frac{1}{2}$ points (spread over three subjects); at one university the average was $11\frac{1}{2}$, at another only 8.

Since the new creations of 1961-7 no further new universities have been established, except an independent one, which will get no money from the state. But in the early 1970s two other new forms of higher education were established. First, thirty of the technical colleges became 'polytechnics'—more than half of them in cities with universities. They are still run by local authorities, but may devise their own courses and examinations for degrees awarded by the authority of the Council for National Academic Awards, once that body (set up in 1964) has given its approval. Their courses (not all technical, and not all leading to degrees) are of many kinds, including part-time and 'sandwich' (interrupted by periods outside). Their popularity is growing rapidly.

Finally, the most interesting innovation of all is the Open University, whose costs are borne mainly by state funds. Its foundation in 1969 owed much to the personal efforts of Harold Wilson as Prime Minister at that time. By 1978 it had 50,000 students, most of them currently working at ordinary full-time jobs—though every imaginable section of the community was included. The University's full-time staff devise courses which they present on one of the B.B.C's television channels and by radio. They have also produced a whole library of short course-books, which anyone can buy at major bookshops or by post from the Open University's centre at the new town of Milton Keynes. Students work with tutors all over the country. Most of the local tutors work part-time; some are for most of their time lecturers in ordinary universities. Students write papers based on the courses, and discuss them with their tutors at meetings or by correspondence. There are also short residential courses in the summer, which students and local tutors attend with great enthusiasm. When the great experiment was inaugurated it was intended that no formal qualifications for admission should be required. But soon applicants were so numerous that some restrictions, including preparatory tests, had to be imposed.

The newest university institution is the University College of

Buckingham, founded in 1976 by some distinguished academics
who were dissatisfied with the dependence of the ordinary
universities on state funds. It is financed by fees and private
contributions, and it has no official recognition. In 1977 it had
nearly 200 students.

Although the universities continued to expand until the late
1970s, there was no dilution of the high ratio of teachers to
students, which remained at about one to ten. The close contact
between them which this made possible was seen as a great merit of
the British system. But from 1976 governments have become more
concerned than before about the high cost to the state, and the
universities have ceased to expand. Tuition fees were raised
progressively. Students from families with moderate incomes could

Students demonstrating for higher university grants.

still have their fees and living costs paid through grants from their home county or borough councils, but the cost of study rose sharply for high income families, and above all for students coming to Britain from other countries.

In the 1980s, state grants to universities were reduced. Older lecturers were encouraged to retire early, and most of those who did retire were not replaced. In 1983 the universities took in slightly fewer students than before, and were forced to become obsessed with the need to cut their costs. Meanwhile, the students in their turn helped the teachers to maintain confidence in their academic work. There were almost no student disruptions such as those of the late 1960s.

Soon the drive for economy affected the educational system as a whole, and in 1984 the Secretary of State for Education began to propose innovations designed specifically to prepare young people for life in the outside world.

Number of teachers and pupil/teacher ratio				
	teachers (thousands)		pupils per teacher	
	1971	1982	1971	1982
State schools				
Primary	203	214	28	22
Secondary	200	280	18	16
Total	403	494	23	19
Private schools				
(all ages)	39	41	14	12

Question

Should Britain aim to bring the pupil/teacher ratio in the state sector down to that in the private sector? What about the cost, in relation to other claims on the economy as a whole?

Number of full-time students in Britain				
	thousands			
	males		females	
	1970-71	1981-82	1970-71	1981-82
University: first degree	128	146	57	99
post-graduate	24	20	8	11
Other higher education	102	124	113	105
UK residents: total	254	290	178	215
Overseas students: total				
(all courses)	20	38	1	4

Questions

1. After three decades of increase, the proportion of the population receiving higher education is stabilising. Do you expect it to start rising again?

2. Note that the proportion of women students is increasing. Do you expect to see more women in leading positions in politics and economic life in the future?

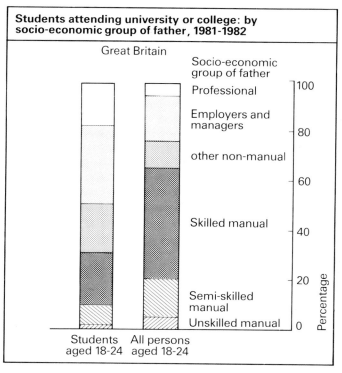

Question

What conclusions do you draw from this chart?

Above: The Anglican cathedral at Salisbury.
Below: The new Roman Catholic cathedral in Liverpool.

11

Religion

British people are perhaps less religious than most others, but religion is now, as it has always been, an important factor in the national life. There is, of course, complete religious freedom, and anyone may belong to any religious faith that he chooses or to none at all. The Church of England is the established Church of the English nation, though perhaps a quarter of the people belong to other religious denominations and many others cannot be said to have any religious attachment. The established Church of Scotland is quite separate, having a different organisation without bishops, and in Wales there is (since 1914) no established Church at all. Nevertheless, it is natural and appropriate to concentrate mainly on the Church of England. The Queen is its head and was crowned, like her predecessors, by the Archbishop of Canterbury in Westminster Abbey. The establishment is part of the law, and important changes concerning the church cannot be made without the consent of Parliament—though many people in the Church wish that this were not so.

First of all, something must be said on definitions. In England the terms 'Anglican Church' and 'Church of England' are almost interchangeable. But there are also other Churches of the same type, and sharing the same origins and the same apostolic succession, outside England. In Scotland and the U.S.A. these churches are called 'Episcopal' or 'Protestant Episcopal', but it is also quite common in these other countries to use the term 'Anglican', meaning in this case apparently 'like the Church of England'. So the particular form of Christianity which has been adopted by England as a nation is also a world-wide form, though outside England it loses its English national character.

The immediate occasion of the Church of England's separation from Rome was political, not doctrinal. King Henry VIII wanted to be rid of his childless wife so that he could remarry. By 1533 a series of Acts of Parliament enabled him to do so. He was now, as King, head of the Church, and his wish was gratified. At first the beliefs and worship of the national Church remained unchanged, but before Henry died he ordered English-language Bibles to be placed in all churches and made accessible to all. In 1549, two years after his death, the use of a newly-devised English-language prayer-book for Church services was made compulsory. After a period of uncomfortable change, stability was reached under Queen Elizabeth, daughter of the Queen whom Henry had married in 1533 and beheaded three years later.

The doctrinal foundation of the Church of England was set out in the Thirty-Nine Articles, agreed by a convention of clergy in 1562 and ratified in 1571. They were England's own national equivalent to the Confession of Augsburg, and included explicit and vehement rejection of 'Romish doctrines' concerning Transubstantiation, Purgatory, invocation of Saints, etc. But bishops were retained, appointed by the Crown. The settlement was protestant yet avoided clear definitions; above all it was English, and a symbol of the nation's insistence on its distinctness.

Another great reform of the sixteenth century allowed priests of the Church of England to be married, and today the clergyman's wife is a most valuable helper in his work. But the Church has still not accepted the idea of having women as priests. There are, however, nearly fifty Anglican religious orders for women, besides a few for men.

Anglican clergymen are ordained, first as deacons and then, after a year, as priests, by bishops, who now follow the advice of the Central Advisory Council for the Training of the Ministry with regard to qualifications. An intending clergyman must normally attend a theological college for at least two years, and many have university degrees, not necessarily in theology. Not long ago most clergymen were of middle to upper class origin, but there is now a rather wider spread, and quite a large number of men become clergymen late in life.

England is divided into parishes, each of which has its incumbent (called either rector or vicar), and there are about 10,000 of these. A vicar is said to have a 'living'. He is not paid by the state, but each living has its financial resources, and the Church has central funds which may be used to help to pay clergymen's stipends, now mostly not above the average worker's income. Each parish has a

patron, who has the right to appoint the vicar, subject to the
bishop's approval, but may not remove him. The patron may be a
private person or a bishop or a college or a society. The vicar works
with his churchwardens and parochial council, and his church is the
centre of many activities, in which he and his wife are the key
figures, much engaged in many aspects of the life of their local
community. For some of these activities they must use their home,
the 'vicarage'. Most of the ten-room vicarages built in the
eighteenth and nineteenth centuries have been sold to well-paid
professional or commercial people; today's vicars live in ordinary
modern small houses.

One clear indication of the Church of England's position as the
national Church is its great architectural heritage. From the
eleventh century until the Reformation the creative genius of the
English was devoted mainly to the building of churches. The great
cathedrals were built in this period, and also hundreds of glorious
parish churches which are still in use. Taken together the medieval
churches are modern England's greatest possession. All these
buildings are now Anglican churches, and this fact identifies the
Anglican Church, rather than any of the other religious
denominations, with the continuity of the nation, of its life and its
traditions. But the state does not make itself responsible for the
physical upkeep of the buildings, and the Church itself has to bear a
heavy financial burden from its own resources and from voluntary
contributions.

England is divided into forty-two dioceses, each with a bishop.
Every diocese has a cathedral as its central church, though the
bishop is concerned with the diocese and its parishes and not with
the cathedral in particular. Each of the great old cathedrals has a
dean and five or six residentiary canons (collectively called dean and
chapter) who are together responsible for the cathedral and its
services. There is often also a choir school, whose boys, together
with the lay clerks, or men of the choir, provide fine music at
matins and evensong each day. The canons live in elegant houses
round the cathedral 'close'; some of them may also hold office as
archdeacons, with administrative responsibilities in the diocese.
Bishops are appointed by the Queen, who acts, in this as in all other
matters, on the Prime Minister's advice. Long ago, Prime Ministers
used this power 'politically' but now they have little reason for
doing so. In 1975 a new system was introduced whereby the Prime
Minister is advised by a committee, with representatives of the

diocese and of the central body of the Church. As he has the constitutional responsibility for what he tells the Queen, he is not obliged to take notice of the Church's wishes, but it can safely be assumed that he does so. The two Archbishops, of Canterbury and York, and 24 senior bishops have seats in the House of Lords, but rarely go there. When the Lords debate a moral or social issue at least one bishop normally speaks, expressing a Christian rather than a party point of view. The bishops have been on the 'liberal' side on issues such as birth control and abortion, and have vigorously opposed all racial discrimination.

In the mid-nineteenth century a quite serious difference developed, among clergy and laity alike, between evangelical and anglo-Catholic sections of the Church. Colloquially called 'low-church' and 'high-church' respectively, these two wings always kept enough tolerant good humour to prevent their rivalry from seriously damaging the Church's unity. The Church of England has produced and tolerated so much eccentricity that it is unlikely ever to be bigoted about liturgy or doctrine.

The rivalry between 'high' and 'low' Church lasted more than a hundred years, but faded out in the 1970s. Michael Ramsey, an academic theologian regarded as an anglo-Catholic, was consecrated as Archbishop of Canterbury in 1961, but devoted himself to the pursuit of Christian unity. Within the Anglican Church old rivalries faded away. The next step was to end the separation from other Protestants on one side and from the Roman Catholic Church on the other. An attempt to achieve union with the Methodists, on the Protestant side, almost succeeded in 1969, but the majority in Church Assembly fell short of the necessary 75%. Ramsey was succeeded in 1975 by Frederick Coggan. He was commonly regarded as an evangelical, but he too devoted himself to the pursuit of union, particularly with Rome. Pope Paul VI's rigidity over birth control and abortion seemed likely to be a merely temporary obstacle, but by 1978 a new difficulty was in sight. The 'Anglican' Church in the United States already had women priests. Most Anglicans in England were convinced that opposition to all discrimination against individuals on grounds such as race must logically involve rejection of discrimination on grounds of sex as well. But the Roman Catholic Church seemed still to be a long way from any prospect of acceptance of women as priests. The Church of England wanted women priests but it had worked hard and long to overcome obstacles to union with Rome.

If the Church of England were to insist on introducing sexual equality in the priesthood it would create an unnecessary new obstacle to that union with Rome which seemed to be quite near to being achieved—and it would endanger the formal union already achieved with the Greek Orthodox Church.

By 1978 the Church of England was moving towards a new division between those ready to sacrifice the prospect of female ordination, so as to protect the hopes of making links with non-protestant Churches, and those who now firmly believed that the exclusion of women from the priesthood should be ended as a matter of principle.

For several decades until the 1970s it had been easy to criticise the Church of England both for its links with the Establishment and for its own internal rivalries. By the 1980s it was suffering more from indifference than from criticism. Neighbouring parishes were being amalgamated, for lack of clergy—and though the number of clergymen was declining there was too little money to support even the reduced number. On any ordinary Sunday no more than 5% of the population went to its services. Four-fifths of the people never went to church at all; more than half of all marriages took place outside church. Adherence to the Church, though by no means dead, had, in spite of the Church's own efforts, become a tolerated interest of a small minority.

Protestants not belonging to the Church of England suffered much persecution in the seventeenth century, and were excluded from many offices and places, including the House of Commons, until the early nineteenth century; in those days they were called 'dissenters', but later the rather more polite term 'nonconformist' came to be used instead. Today the still more polite term 'members of the Free Churches' is more usual, except among the more intolerant Anglicans. Of the old dissenting sects, the Baptists and the United Reformed Church (consisting of the Congregational and Presbyterian Churches who merged in 1972), are perhaps the most important, though many Presbyterians in England are in fact Scottish people who have taken their own religion southwards across the border. The Quakers have always been a very small and select group, and have their meeting-houses, for the most part, only in large towns; but they are immensely respected and in general rather wealthy. There are many other Protestant sects also, some strong in one town, some strong in another.

More important, in the matter of numbers, than any of these old sects are the Methodists, who follow the movement started by John Wesley in the eighteenth century. He was ordained as a clergyman of the Church of England in 1725, and taught and preached at Oxford for some years, becoming the central figure in a small group who were called 'Methodists' and tried to live a deeply religious life together. After some time in the American colony of Georgia, where he was regarded as a rigid High Churchman, he began to preach in many places in England, and 1739 is considered as the beginning of the Methodist societies, which soon grew up all over the country. Wesley and his followers were religious enthusiasts. They had no objection to the doctrine of the Church of England, but found it indifferent to its Christian duties and to the needs of the ordinary people. It was also indifferent or hostile to Wesley. He travelled over the country preaching often in the open air, and soon had an immense following. In time many Methodist churches were built and regular preachers and ministers were appointed. The evangelical revival in the Church of England was a belated response to the needs which Wesley had seen earlier, but by then Methodism had already become very important and is probably now the main religion of the people in many northern mining and industrial areas and also in Wales, though the Welsh form is distinct from the English. English Methodists have a regular form of church service and an organisation based on 'circuits'. They also make much use of lay preachers. The number of ministers—4,000—is about half that of the Anglican beneficed clergy. They have suffered various divisions but were reunited, except for the Independent Methodists, in 1932. One great follower of Wesley's path was William Booth, founder of the Salvation Army. Its brass bands play hymn-tunes in the streets on Sundays, and its officers do admirable social work.

The Roman Catholic Church was persecuted and weak in England for a long time after the Reformation. Its English hierarchy was extinct from the sixteenth century until 1850, but now England and Wales have four archbishops and fourteen bishops. The number of Roman Catholics seems to be growing, and there is a trickle of converts, including a fair number of intellectuals. Many of the Roman Catholics in England are the descendants of immigrants from Ireland, which has always remained predominantly Roman Catholic, and it is sometimes said that Roman Catholic priests are among the main Irish exports to England.

There is no 'Christian' political party and no anti-religious or anti-clerical party either. On the whole Conservatism and adherence to the Church of England tend to go together, though many Anglicans vote against the Conservatives and many members of other denominations vote for them. But the Conservatives regard themselves as a 'national' party, and the Church of England has a special attraction for them because it is identified with the nation. It is significant that the term 'the Establishment' in its modern use is taken from the older, more particular sense connected with the Church. The Church of England, and particularly its hierarchy, is the very centre of the old Establishment, while the Free Churches, from their origins, have been outside and opposed to the whole idea.

In politics both nineteenth-century liberalism and modern socialism have their roots partly in nonconformist Protestantism. Among Labour Members of Parliament, particularly those who have worked as coal-miners before being elected, there are many who had their first experience of public speaking and of social leadership in their local Methodist churches and church activities. While the intellectual element among Labour Party politicians is perhaps mainly agnostic, many of the working men who have come up through the trade unions are Free Church Protestants. Among Roman Catholic congregations, particularly in the big cities, there are large numbers of Labour Party supporters, though there are also some English Catholics who are to be counted as among the most right-wing of Conservatives.

Since the early nineteenth century religion has been the chief inspiration of the immense amount of work for good causes, which is so much in evidence in England. Innumerable organisations have been built up by voluntary effort for the purpose of helping the poor, the old, the sick, young people and other groups who seem to need sympathetic care, and very many of these organisations have a religious origin. English social life cannot be understood without some reference to this great volume of unpaid service, of expenditure of money and effort, on behalf of all sorts of altruistic causes. Much of this work is connected with particular churches and regarded as an expression of Christian duty in the world.

During the last part of the nineteenth century and the earlier part of the twentieth, religion had great effects on social life and behaviour, some of which are still evident. The vigorously Protestant elements, both in the Church of England and outside it, were very active in the fight against the more obvious forms of sin. Such people hated all self-indulgence and promoted state action to suppress it. The laws restricting drinking and gambling, and forbidding many activities on Sundays, are in part the product of a Protestant spirit which continued the old Puritan tradition, with its condemnation of the pursuit of pleasure and its insistence on hard work and self-sacrifice. But this attitude, in its more rigorous forms, is much more rare today; the people who criticise the Duke of Edinburgh for playing polo on Sundays are only a tiny minority.

It is difficult to produce any reliable statistics of religious observance; there are people who go to church regularly, others who go occasionally, and others who enter a church only for baptisms, weddings and funerals. There are in England about 3,000,000 Roman Catholics, most of whom do go to church regularly, about 2,000,000 members of Free Churches (including over 1,000,000 Methodists), and 400,000 Jews. Most of the others, if they were asked their religious affiliation, would probably say 'Church of England'. In recent years about a quarter of all young English people have been confirmed as full members of the Anglican Church. But confirmed members of the Church of England are told that they ought to go to Communion on Easter Sunday, and the number who do this is about two million people or five per cent of the adult English population. About a third of all marriages are held in Anglican churches, and a third of all babies are baptised. On an ordinary Sunday, about two per cent of adults attend a service of the Church of England, including both regulars and those who go five or ten times a year. According to various surveys, on any ordinary Sunday in the past twenty years, more people have been to Catholic church services than to all Protestant services combined. The Anglicans' decline seems now to have been halted, while the main old established free churches have continued to lose support. The Methodists have lost more than half of their membership in the past twenty years. Meanwhile some newer, smaller groups are flourishing. Jehovah's Witnesses and Mormons claim nearly 100,000 members each. Many old Methodist or Presbyterian chapels in cities have been taken over by new groups, or by immigrant congregations (including some from Eastern Europe who have settled in certain areas of London and other cities).

Because of immigration from the Indian sub-continent, there are now important communities of Moslems, Hindus, Sikhs and adherents of other eastern religions. The greatest newly-built place of worship in Britain is the impressive London Mosque by the edge of Regent's Park.

Television and radio give time for broadcasts of religious services, carefully distributed according to supposed demand. Some of these are ecumenical; great occasions like the marriage of the Prince of Wales, and the visit of Pope John Paul II, have lately involved participation of several religious groups, watched with enthusiasm on TV by the majority of the population. But almost all regular religious life goes on in a local context, not positively exclusive but not much concerned about the dividing lines between religious bodies.

Religious participation					
	thousands				
	membership		adults attending church		per cent of adult population attending church
	1975	1979	1975	1979	1979
Church of England	2000	1900	1300	1250	3.6
Methodist	515	473	454	447	1.3
Baptist	168	162	193	203	0.6
United Reformed	190	166	150	139	0.4
Other Protestant	360	400	320	380	1.1
Roman Catholic	3513	3530	1418	1310	3.7

Question

In view of the fact that less than eleven per cent of the adult population attend any church, what basis do you think there is for calling Britain a Christian country?

The large selection of newspapers and magazines available at any newsagent's.

12

The Press, Radio and Television

1 Daily and Sunday Papers

British people buy more newspapers than any others except the Swedes and Japanese. Most of the daily papers belong to one of five big companies, which also have financial interests in television and are sometimes called 'empires'. The press differs in two obvious ways from that of any similar European country. First, all over England most people read 'national' papers, based in London, which altogether sell more copies than all the eighty-odd provincial papers combined. Second, there is a striking difference between the four 'quality' papers and the five mass-circulation popular tabloids.

These characteristics are still more salient with the Sunday press. Almost no papers at all are published in England on Sundays except 'national' ones; four 'popular' and three 'quality', based in London. Three of these appear on Sundays only; four others are associated with dailies which have the same names but different editors and journalists and different layouts. The 'quality' Sunday papers devote large sections to literature and the arts. They have colour supplements and are in many ways more like magazines than newspapers. They supply quite different worlds of taste and interest from the 'popular' papers.

Scotland has two important 'quality' papers, the *Scotsman* in Edinburgh and the *Glasgow Herald*. The Glasgow *Daily Record* survives: two other 'popular' papers have disappeared. On Sundays the *Sunday Post,* of Dundee, claims to be read by four-fifths of the Scottish population. Scotland's cultural distinctness is reflected in its press.

The national uniformity and the difference between 'quality' and 'mass' papers together correspond with and reflect both the weakness of regional identity and the gulf between the social classes. With the press, people in all parts of England choose one or

THE PRINCIPAL NEWSPAPERS

A. Papers based in London but circulating nationwide

Quality	Political tendency	Circulation 000's	Sunday equivalent	Circulation 000's
Times	Ind (Con)	350	Sunday Times	1,300
Guardian	Ind (Liberal)	450	—	
Daily Telegraph	Conservative	1,300	Sunday Telegraph	700
Financial Times	Ind (Con)	200	—	
—			Observer	700
Popular				
Daily Mail	Con	2,000	Mail on Sunday	1,500
Daily Express	Con	2,000	Sunday Express	3,000
Daily Mirror	Lab	3,500	Sunday Mirror	4,000
Daily Star	Con	1,400	—	
Sun	Con	4,200	News of the World	6,000
Morning Star	Communist	60	—	
—			Sunday People	4,000

B. Regional papers

(London) Standard	Con	1,500 (belongs to Daily Express)
16 Morning papers	Ind	2,000 in all
70 Evening papers	Ind	7,000 in all

more of the eight national papers according to their preferences which are based on various factors, among which national sport reports are probably more influential than politics, and certainly more influential than anything to do with the region.

The gap in quality is not so much between Labour and Conservative, as between levels of ability to read and appreciate serious news presented seriously. Of the four quality morning papers only the *Telegraph* is solidly Conservative; nearly all the *Telegraph*'s readers are Conservatives. *The Times* and *Financial Times* have a big minority of non-Conservative readers. Of the popular papers the *Mail, Sun, Daily Star* and *Express* are solidly Conservative, the *Mirror* regularly Labour. Plenty of Labour voters read popular papers with Conservative inclinations, but do not change their minds because of what they have read. Some of them are interested only in the human interest stories and in sport, and may well hardly notice the reporting of political and economic affairs.

Most of the significant regional newspapers are 'evening' papers, each publishing about four editions between about mid-day and 5 p.m. London like every other important town has one. All these 'evening' papers are semi-popular, but none has a circulation approaching that of any popular national paper.

The national press is dominated by large companies, some of which have other interests besides, in commercial television or Canadian forests—even in package holidays or North Sea oil. A national newspaper needs a strong financial base.

In one sense the national press may seem enormously successful. Its total daily sales in England amount to 13 million, or three papers sold for every four households. Yet their financial position is not at all successful. Most of the national papers have lost money in the 1970s, and their financial difficulties were not resolved by the 1980s. Most lost circulation in this period, partly because of severe price-increases caused by the heavy cost of production and distribution. Attempts to cut their costs by using more efficient production processes have caused several strikes. In 1976–84 all the London national papers had some periods when they were not published.

The question of possible subsidies from the state is often raised, but the arguments against subsidy have prevailed. One of the most powerful of all British traditions is that of free speech, and particularly free criticism of the Government, along with freedom to demand information which the Government would prefer to suppress. The press itself has felt that any help or even privilege granted by the state would spoil its reputation for independence, even if the state managed not to interfere.

Curiously, by 1976 there was a new threat to editoral independence, involving the state in a new and unexpected way. The Labour Party, then in office, and itself supported mainly by trade unions, was busily promoting laws to extend union power. Part of one bill seemed to threaten editorial freedom by enabling unions to exert influence over the editors' choice of writers and even over what should be printed and what should not. After a long battle, in which the House of Lords involved itself, an uncertain compromise was found.

Although the newspapers receive no money from the state (and partly because of this) they rely heavily on revenues from advertisers. A mass-circulation national newspaper, selling two or more million copies in every corner of the country, is not a suitable vehicle for advertisements of ordinary jobs or houses or cars for sale in south London or in Manchester. It must rely mainly on advertisements from large manufacturers or package-holiday firms with nationwide selling networks. It is often suggested that newspapers do not print either reports or comment which might displease their major advertisers; that their freedom from the state makes them dependent on big business and subservient to its interest. It is easy to make assertions of this kind, but harder to find evidence to support them. On the contrary, newspapers can quote countless instances where they have criticised big firms which have advertised in them before and after criticism. Yet, at a more subtle level, some element of doubt remains. Investigative reporting, in pursuit of stories usually exposing abuse of power, is difficult and expensive. It takes courage for an editor to invest heavily in an investigation which may well fail to produce results, and whose results, if any, might annoy the advertisers. Nevertheless, some editors have shown that courage, and their papers have not suffered from it.

At a lower level it is also true that, for example, the writers of the motoring columns do not criticise the fundamental assumptions of car-manufacturers. They do not suggest that it is silly to make cars capable of going 200 kilometres an hour on roads where the speed limit is 110. They do not suggest that new fashions are silly and wasteful. Probably they don't make such suggestions because they would themselves emphatically deny them. But that is because the newspapers give jobs as columnists writing about cars or aviation or clothes-fashion to people who share the values of those who produce those things.

On balance, it seems unfair to criticise the press, particularly the national press, for subservience to the commercial interests of their main advertisers. Its courage outweighs its caution, though it is probably weak in imaginative initiative over minor or specialist issues. Even the quality papers are reluctant to tire their readers with heavily detailed fact and argument about matters which lack political 'sex-appeal'. This fact may well be illustrated by the extreme feebleness of the reporting of foreign news except catastrophes or crimes or major economic trends or big party-political events.

The 'popular' newspapers respond to their estimates of their readers' interests. They use enormous headlines for the leading items of each day, which are one day political, one day to do with crime, one day sport, one day some odd happening. They have their pages of political report and comment, short, often over-simplified but vigorously written and (nowadays) generally responsible. They thrive on sensational stories and excitement.

The two archetypal popular papers, the *Daily Mail* and *Daily Express*, were both built up by individual tycoons in the early twentieth century. Both had a feeling for the taste of a newly-literate public: if a man bites a dog, that's news. The *Express* was built up by a man born in poverty in Canada. He built up his newspaper in Britain, not only on crime and human interest stories, but on his simple message about the greatness of the British Empire. He became a great man in the land, a close friend and associate of Winston Churchill, a powerful minister in his war Cabinet. The circulation of the *Express* at one time exceeded 4 million copies a day. Now the first Lord Beaverbrook is dead, the paper is searching for a new identity, and the daily sales are not much more than half of their highest figure. The history of the *Daily Mail*, with its more conventional conservatism, is not greatly different. Both of these papers have become 'tabloids' (printed on smaller sheets of paper) within the past ten years.

The Communist Party's *Morning Star* might well be placed beside the *Express* and *Mail*. But the *Morning Star's* circulation is said to be about 60,000—only a small fraction of that of any other national paper; most people would scarcely regard it as a national paper at all. It supports all strikes, condemns all the social evils it can find—and sells more copies in Eastern Europe (where it is the only permitted British paper) than in Britain.

In popular journalism the *Daily Mirror* became a serious rival of the *Express* and *Mail* in the 1940s. It was always tabloid, always devoted more space to pictures. It was also a pioneer with strip cartoons. During the war it was the Government's fiercest and most effective critic, and at one time Churchill was tempted to use the Government's special wartime powers to suppress it. He was indeed sorely tempted; but he left it free. After 1945 it regularly supported the Labour Party. It soon outdid the *Express* in size of headlines, short sentences and exploitation of excitement. It also became the biggest-selling daily newspaper. For many years its sales have been above 4 million; sometimes well above.

In the mid 1970s the *Mirror's* daily sales were slightly exceeded by those of a new paper, *The Sun*, whose achievement was built on nudity and even bigger headlines. It is the successor of the old *Daily Herald* which until the 1960s was a quasi-official organ of the Labour Party. After several changes of status and ownership *The Sun* was taken over by Mr Rupert Murdoch, whose first big newspapers were in Australia. Before his firm took over *The Sun* it already owned the *News of the World*, a British Sunday paper which pays special attention to reports of crimes and whose sales once exceeded 8 million copies.

Journalists working for the popular papers, in their competition for stories to satisfy the public's interest in crime and scandal, are tempted to intrude unscrupulously into the private lives of citizens who happen to be connected with such events. In the 1950s, one innocent victim of some intolerable day-and-night intrusion wrote an eloquent letter to *The Times*. His complaints had some influence. A semi-independent quasi-court, The Press Council, was set up. Its Chairman is normally a distinguished lawyer or academic. In 1978 its membership was increased to 36, half to represent various press interests, half specially appointed from outside the field.

Any person who has a grievance against a newspaper may bring a complaint to the Press Council, which considers the evidence on both sides and makes a report, which may either exonerate an editor or journalist or criticise a failure to observe reasonable standards of journalistic behaviour. In twenty years the Press Council has built up, through its reports, a body of principles both positive and negative. Once a local official committee held a series of private meetings about a plan to close a major local industrial plant. A journalist gained access to information which was meant to be confidential. His editor decided that the plans concerned the public interest and published the information. The Press Council received a complaint but rejected it, on the ground that there was neither law nor overriding public interest to make the publication inappropriate. But the Council has criticised journalists for failing to respect private lives, and its adverse reports, though carrying no formal penalty, have discouraged excessive zeal in taking photographs in such a way as to cause pointless embarrassment or distress to innocent people.

The Times is the most famous of all British newspapers, and has always been the paper of the 'Establishment', who use it for

announcements of births, marriages and deaths. In 1981 it was taken
over by the Murdoch group, though its editoral independence was
guaranteed. Politically it is independent but inclined to be
sympathetic to the Conservative Party. It is not an organ of the
Government. Sometimes its leading articles, on the right-hand side
of the centre pages, may be written after private consultation with
people in, for example, the Foreign Office; but they are often
critical of any government. It has a reputation for caution in its
attitudes, and this reputation is on the whole deserved. The letters
to the Editor, which are printed next to the leading articles, are
very influential, and may lead to wide discussion of the views
which they express.

   The Guardian was called the *Manchester Guardian* until 1959, and
the change in name indicates its success in becoming more and
more a truly national paper. Later it moved its base to London. In
quality, style and reporting it is equal with *The Times*; in politics it
is perhaps best described as 'radical'. It is more favourable to the
Liberal Party than to the Conservatives. It has made great progress
during the past thirty years, particularly among intelligent people
who find *The Times* too uncritical of established interests.

   The *Daily Telegraph* is theoretically independent, but in practice
very close to being an organ of the Conservative Party. Well
produced and edited and full of real information, it deserves to be
considered as belonging to the same class of journalism as *The
Times* and *The Guardian*. It contains much more reading matter
than the popular papers. Its circulation is twice as great as that of
The Times and *The Guardian* together; this may be partly because its
price is lower.

   The *Financial Times* has recently shed its old commercial
specialism and has become a major quality paper, enjoying a
reputation rivalling *The Times*. Its circulation, though small, has
grown enormously. Its success in recent years has rivalled the *Sun's*
at the opposite end of the scale.

   Although the quality papers sell altogether only one-sixth as
many copies as the mass-circulation populars, they have increased
their share of the total market since 1950. On Sundays, the quality
Sunday Times and *Observer* together sold less than a million copies
in 1950 (compared with the popular Sundays' 25 million). By 1984
although they had dropped by 10% since 1970, they (together with
the new *Sunday Telegraph*) sold $2\frac{1}{2}$ million copies between them,
compared with the populars' 18 million. The 'quality' share of the

Sunday market has risen from less than one in twenty to one in seven. The spread of education seems to have had some effect.

2   Local and Regional Papers

Local morning papers have suffered from the universal penetration of the London-based national press. Only sixteen survive in the whole of England, and their combined circulation is much less than that of the *Sun* alone. Among local daily papers those published in the evenings are much more important. Each of seventy towns has one, selling only within a radius of 50 to 100 kilometres. The two London evening papers, the *News* and *Standard*, together sold two million copies in 1980, but they could not both survive, and merged into one, now called *The Standard*.

Most local daily papers belong to one or other of the big press empires, which leave their local editors to decide editorial policy. Mostly they try to avoid any appearance of regular partisanship, giving equal weight to each major political party. They give heavy weight to local news and defend local interests and local industries. A Bristol paper must vigorously support the Concorde aircraft, which is built in Bristol.

A European visitor to Britain may be surprised to see no kiosks on the pavements. Some people buy their morning or evening papers in shops, others have them brought to their homes not by the mail service but by boys or girls who want to earn money by doing 'paper-rounds'. In towns evening papers are sold by elderly men who stand for four hours on the pavement, stamping their feet to keep warm.

The total circulation of all the provincial daily newspapers, morning and evening together, is around 8 million: about half as great as that of the eight national papers. In spite of this, some provincial papers are quite prosperous. They do not need their own foreign correspondents; they receive massive local advertising, particularly of things for sale; some (not all) of them have persuaded their printing staffs to accept the efficient production-methods which the London unions will not accept on any reasonable terms. If a national paper's compositors refuse to work new machines unless each man is paid larger wages, that national paper's costs must rise beyond reasonable limits. London's ascendancy may well not endure.

The truly local papers are weekly. They are not taken very

seriously, being mostly bought for the useful information contained in their advertisements. But for a foreign visitor wishing to learn something of the flavour of a local community, the Friday local paper can be useful.

Most of the daily and weekly newspapers are owned by large companies which also own national papers, as well as large shares in the regional commercial television companies. The dominance of these few big firms in the whole world of public information is often criticised, but they have become sensitive to the criticism and take care to avoid giving cause for complaint.

3   The Weekly and Periodical Press

Good English writing is often to be found in the weekly political and literary journals, all based in London, all with nationwide circulations in the tens of thousands. *The Economist*, founded in 1841, probably has no equal anywhere. It has recently adopted a coloured cover, and has a few photographs inside, so that it looks like *Time* and *Newsweek*, *Der Spiegel* and *l'Express*, but its reports have more depth and breadth than any of these. It covers the world's affairs, and even its American section is more informative about America than its American equivalents. Although by no means 'popular', it is vigorous in its comments, and deserves the respect in which it is universally held. Its circulation rose in the 1970s, and reached 240,000 in 1984—more than half outside Britain. The *New Statesman* and *Spectator* are weekly journals of opinion, one left, one right. They regularly contain well-written articles, often politically prejudiced. Both devote nearly half their space to literature and the arts. Both lost circulation after other weeklies had disappeared.

The Times has three weekly '*Supplements*', all published separately. The *Literary Supplement* is devoted almost entirely to book reviews and covers all kinds of new literature. It makes good use of academic contributors, and has at last, unlike the *Economist*, abandoned its old tradition of anonymous reviews. The Times *Educational* and *Higher Education* Supplements are obviously specialist, and useful sources for any serious student of these fields of interest. *New Society* and *New Scientist*, both published by the company which owns the *Daily Mirror*, sometimes have good and serious articles about sociological and scientific research, often written by academics yet useful for the general reader.

One old British institution, the satirical weekly *Punch*, survives, more abrasive than in an earlier generation yet finding it hard to keep the place it once had in a more secure social system. Its attraction, particularly for the intellectual youth, has been surpassed by a new rival, *Private Eye*, founded in 1962 by people who, not long before, had run a pupils' magazine in Shrewsbury School. It is so scurrilous that some main chains of newsagents will not sell it, but its scandalous material is admirably written on atrocious paper and its circulation rivals that of the *Economist*.

Glossly weekly or monthly picture magazines cater either for women or for any of a thousand special interests. Almost all are based in London, with national circulations, and the women's magazines sell millions of copies, encouraging people to buy new wallpapers, carpets and equipment for their kitchens—and, of course, new clothes. These, along with commercial television, are the great educators of demand for the new and better goods offered by the modern consumer-society. In any big newsagent's shop the long rows of brightly covered magazines seem to go on for ever; beyond the infinite variety of appeals to housewives, mothers, brides and teenagers come those concerned with yachting, tennis, model railways, gardening and cars. For every activity with any human following, there is a magazine, supported mainly by its advertisers, and from time to time the police bring a pile of pornographic magazines to local magistrates, who have the difficult task of deciding whether they are offensive.

These specialist papers are not cheap. They live off an infinite variety of taste, ambition, desire to know, create and buy. Their production, week by week and month by month, represents a fabulous amount of effort, along with the felled trees of Swedish and Canadian forests. Television has not killed the desire to read.

4 Radio and Television

When the spread of radio began, the British were quick to agree on certain principles. Unlike the press, it should not be financed, even partially, through commercial advertising; but its programmes should be free from state control, and should therefore have no state subsidy. The British Broadcasting Corporation (B.B.C.) was set up, given the monopoly of radio broadcasting, and financed by compulsory annual payments. The Minister in charge of Posts and Telecommunications appoints the B.B.C.'s Board of Governors and its chairman. The qualifications for these positions are not precisely defined, but it has from the beginning been accepted that the Minister should not use his power so as to give politicians of his own party any kind of control in the governing board. The Director-General and staff are appointed on grounds of qualifications and experience, always in such a way as to ensure that there is the least possible ground for allegations of partisanship or bias.

The picture used by I.T.V. to introduce their ten o'clock news bulletin.

A still from an Independent Television advertisement for a well-known brand of drinks.

British television's first channel was run by the B.B.C., financed by an annual charge on viewers and without advertising. In 1963 a second, wholly commercial channel was allowed to start up, and by 1982 there were four channels, two B.B.C. and two commercial, with the new commercial Channel 4 giving some time to minority interests, and with a Welsh language channel covering Wales. With the start of two early morning news and comment programmes in 1983, television was running for 16 to 18 hours each day, and received by 97 per cent of all households.

On sound the B.B.C runs four programmes; '1' for pop music, '2' for light entertainment, '3' for minority interests, including music. For part of the day it is used for the academic courses of the

Open University. The main programme for news, comment and discussion is B.B.C. Radio 4, which (unlike the others) is split into separate regional programmes for part of the day. There are also locally-run B.B.C. programmes such as Radio Bristol, and, since 1973, some local commercial sound broadcasting stations, with mainly music and news.

B.B.C. Television's first channel resembles the fourth radio programme. Except for the short period when it splits into regions, it broadcasts the same news, comment, plays, sports reports, etc., nationwide—though many of its nationwide items are produced by one or another of the regions. The second channel sometimes caters for minority tastes, including occasionally a complete opera. It broadcasts Open University courses outside popular viewing hours.

Although commercial television, financed by advertising, was set up by the Conservative Party against vigorous Labour opposition, the Labour Party soon began to regard it favourably. It was found that most Labour voters preferred it to the B.B.C. The law governing it is complicated; the main points are, first that there are fifteen regional programme companies covering the whole U.K., and second that each regional company decides its own programmes. Advertisers' material appears for one or two minutes at quarter-hour intervals, either between programme-items or in so-called 'natural breaks'. The advertisers do not sponsor the programmes or have any direct influence on their content. However, the charge for each half-minute of time is high, and varies according to the likely number of viewers. The programme companies' financial success depends on their ability to attract viewers, and the programmes themselves inevitably reflect public tastes. The B.B.C. in its turn does not like to be humiliated by loss of viewers to independent television, so it has to compete on the same level.

The fears expressed by Labour Party spokesmen—and by serious journalists, educators, etc.—about the introduction of a commercial element have been only partly realised. One effect of competition is that at one time the viewer can choose between B.B.C 1's western film and the I.T.V's western film, at another time between two rival commentators on the same sporting event.

All four channels produce a good mixture of miscellaneous entertainment, music, drama and serious discussion. All succeed in presenting news efficiently, interestingly and without bias. There are numerous discussion programmes allowing the clash of opposing points of view. One common complaint is of triviality. Because the public can so easily be bored, programmes of political argument and discussion rarely allow anyone to develop any theme in depth. The broadcasts about current problems, particularly on television, are devised so as to enable exponents of different points of view free scope for setting forth their arguments—though there is too much interrupting; and one participant who merely repeats stale slogans is allowed too much time, while another who has a complex case to put is not given the time he needs to develop it.

Both radio and television are often criticised for many and contradictory reasons. But there seems to be a common opinion among people familiar with the productions of several countries that, compared with others, the British still deserve praise. Televised drama is often at a high level, both in the individual items and in long-running weekly series. The B.B.C. and the commercial channels can both, at their best, be excellent; and both spend some time producing rubbish.

Programmes for schools are used extensively by teachers, and other programmes have a clearly educational purpose. The B.B.C., as a state organisation, is more constrained on expenditure, yet probably more inclined to waste resources through top-heavy administrative costs. However, the compulsory contribution to its costs, which has to be paid by every household which owns or hires a television set (£46 for colour, £15 for black and white in 1984) is low by international standards. In 1982 the B.B.C. spent £800 million, and gave good value to its customers.

When Wilson was Prime Minister he complained that the B.B.C. was hostile to him, but Conservative politicians made opposite complaints. In fact, all broadcasting observes rigid rules about impartiality. The two major parties have equal time for their own broadcasts, and both parties of the Alliance have a somewhat smaller share of time (and in Scotland and Wales the Nationalists). All political discussions balance the opposing views against one another.

Newspaper readership by social class: 1982							
	circulation (millions)	social class (percentage)					
		A	B	C1	C2	D	E
Serious (4 papers)	2.2	67	42	19	6	4	1
Semi-popular (2 papers)	3.9	32	34	33	23	19	15
Popular (3 papers)	8.7	14	24	29	52	90	57

Note People who read more than one newspaper are counted for each paper they read.

Question

Do these figures suggest a greater difference in taste between socio-economic classes in Britain than in most other countries?

Above: The steel works at Margam, Port Talbot.
Below: Houses in the new town of Cumbernauld in Scotland.

13

Wales, Scotland and Ireland

1   The United Kingdom

This book is about British institutions, but there is some confusion about the meaning of the word 'Britain'. Properly speaking, Great Britain is the large island which includes England, Scotland and Wales, though the term is usually taken to include the four groups of Scottish islands—the Orkneys and Shetlands, the Inner and Outer Hebrides, which are administered as part of Scotland. The political unit, for government and administration, is properly called 'the United Kingdom of Great Britain and Northern Ireland'. This does not include the southern part of Ireland, which is now an independent republic and not even a member of the Commonwealth, and to be quite accurate it does not include the Channel Islands of Jersey, Guernsey and others, which lie off the coast of Normandy, or the Isle of Man, which lies between England and Ireland. These islands have their own legislatures and administrations and financial systems, but are more closely attached to the United Kingdom than the independent countries of the Commonwealth in other parts of the world.

Wales, Scotland and Northern Ireland, though all part of the United Kingdom, all have their own peculiar relationships with the United Kingdom, and must be discussed separately; Wales is the most closely related with England, and Norhtern Ireland the least closely. Nationalist sentiment has recently become more vigorous in Scotland and Wales, and the central government has made some administrative changes in an attempt to satisfy it. In 1969 a constitutional commission was set up to examine the whole problem of the relations between the parts of the United Kingdom. Its report (1973) proposed further changes.

Already by this time the Scottish National Party suddenly gained significant electoral support in Scotland. Its ultimate aim was separation. With 30% of the votes in Scotland it won only 11 seats out of 71 at the general election of October 1974, but it was clear that a small further gain of votes could well give it more Scottish seats than either the Conservatives or the Labour Party. In Wales the Welsh National Party (Plaid Cymru) showed a smaller gain, but won 3 of the 36 Welsh seats in the U.K. Parliament.

In 1978, after immensely long and controversial debate, Parliament passed two bills making detailed provision for the election of new assemblies in Scotland and Wales, with some legislative powers. In England both major parties were divided on some of the issues. Both Acts of Parliament included a provision, inserted against the Labour government's wishes, that they would come into effect only after being approved by majorities of the registered electorates in Scotland and Wales, with votes of Yes by at least 40 per cent of all those entitled to vote.

The Welsh people decisively rejected the whole scheme. Only 12 per cent of the Welsh electorate voted Yes, 47 per cent No, and 41 per cent did not vote. In Scotland the result was close: 32.85 per cent Yes, 30.78 per cent No. As the small Yes majority was less than 40 per cent of the Scottish electorate, the Act could not be put into effect.

2   Wales

Wales has been united with England for seven hundred years, and through all this time England and Wales have formed one single, undifferentiated political and administrative unit. The son and heir of the monarch is given the title 'Prince of Wales', but his title has no political significance. The Welsh people are predominantly Celtic and have always kept a strong consciousness of their ethnic distinctness. The population of Wales is about 2,700,000, mostly living in the coal-mining and industrial region of the south round Cardiff and Swansea, but many Welsh people have migrated to England and tend to regard themselves as Welsh at least until the second generation.

Almost the whole of Wales is mountainous, with much good scenery. The coal-mining villages of the south are in deep valleys among high hills, and the hills become higher towards the north. The highest mountain in the north, Snowdon, is 3,560 feet (nearly 1,100 metres) above sea level, and is higher than any point in England.

Among the best-known Welsh characteristics are a certain romanticism and love of poetry and music. The annual bardic festival known as the National Eisteddfod of Wales has a 1,200-year-old history; choral singing, and particularly the singing of hymns, is a national art. Oratory is another. It once flourished particularly among Baptist, Methodist and Presbyterian preachers in the chapels which dominate the mining villages. Now the same eloquence is practised more in trade unions and the Labour Party. Another source of national pride is Rugby football. Wales often beats England or France in the annual international matches. This achievement seems remarkable when the populations are compared, but in fact is helped by the identification of the whole population with a game which in the larger countries involves only minorities. The hymn-singing by the spectators towards the end of a victorious match at Cardiff is a sound not easily forgotten.

In politics Welsh was once predominantly Liberal. Now Labour dominates the thickly-populated south. Liberal support has been sustained in the rest of Wales, though by 1974 it suffered through the rise of the Welsh National Party (Plaid Cymru).

Welsh objections to complete political assimilation with England were met, in 1951–75, by a succession of steps by U.K. governments towards devolved administration. Since 1964 the Cabinet has included a Secretary of State for Wales, responsible for roads, schools, planning and local government services. Meanwhile, the Welsh National Party (Plaid Cymru) grew in strength a little. It won about 4% of the votes in Wales in the general elections of 1959–66, but its support trebled by 1970. In the 1970 election its candidates won 11% of the votes in Wales but failed to win any seats in Parliament. The vote declined a little in 1974, but in October it won three seats in the House of Commons; Welsh nationalism achieved some political significance. But the bill for legislative devolution for Wales was rejected so decisively by the Welsh people at the referendum of 1979, that nationalism lost its impetus. Plaid Cymru kept its two seats in 1983, with eight per cent of all votes in Wales. It had one success, with the introduction of a separate Welsh language television channel.

Cultural nationalism, connected with the Welsh language, is strong. Welsh, which is a Celtic language, very different from English, and the only really distinctive national feature, has remained the first language only in some remote westerly country districts, in some of which three-quarters of the people can speak it.

But in the whole of Wales 99% of the people can speak English, and Welsh is in fact declining; at the 1981 census only 19% of all people in Wales claimed to be able to speak Welsh, as compared with 29% in 1951. However, militant enthusiasts for the Welsh language dominate local public life and the local councils, and they are exerting tremendous pressure for the general revival of Welsh-speaking. But two years of compulsory Welsh-learning at school do not get you very far beyond a capacity to pronounce place-names like Troedyrhiw and Cwmrhydyceirw. Meanwhile, very few people dare to resist or even to state the case against this linguistic pressure.

Princes Street, Edinburgh.

3   Scotland

In area, Scotland is more than half as big as England. Its population is, however, only about 5,200,000 or one-eighth as great as that of England. Scotland was an independent kingdom, often at war with England, until 1603. It had never been entirely conquered by the Romans, who advanced some distance into what is now Scotland, but for most of their four centuries in Britain remained mainly behind the great wall which they built in the reign of the Emperor Hadrian, from sea to sea across the island of Great Britain, a little way to the south of the modern boundary between England and Scotland. In 1603 King James VI of Scotland became King of England too, as James I, and from then onwards the countries were under the same monarch, though the Act of Union was not passed until 1707. This Act incorporated Scotland with England in the United Kingdom, but the Scots kept their own legal system, religion and administration and still keep them now. Thus Scotland has never been united with England in the same way as Wales.

On the whole Scottish national consciousness is cultural and sentimental, and not much concerned with language. The Gaelic language, a Celtic form, is still used rather than English among the people of some remote Highland districts, but elsewhere most of the people are not of Celtic origin and would have no possible reason for wanting to introduce the Gaelic language, which would be an entirely foreign tongue. The English language is spoken all over Scotland with a variety of regional accents, but all of these can be at once recognised as Scottish, with the vowels and consonants pronounced more nearly as written than in standard English or any of the regional accents of England. Also, there are many words and phrases which are peculiar to Scottish use, and this is felt to maintain national distinctness quite enough. At the same time, though there is much talk about the Scottish nation, there seems to be a subtle and spontaneous movement towards cultural assimilation with England, with many of the upper classes adopting standard English pronunciation and sending their sons to English public schools and universities. Scottish Presbyterianism is becoming less rigorous and inward-looking, and the annual festival of music and the arts, held in Edinburgh every August for the past thirty years, is truly international in the partly provincial atmosphere of Scotland's grandiose capital city.

Scotland is a northern land, and its climate has often been blamed for a certain hardness attributed to the lowlanders, who form the majority of the inhabitants. This is only partly fair. Scotland is not particularly cold, and the west is in winter one of the mildest parts of Britain. But even in the 'lowlands' much of the land is too high for easy cultivation; most of the hillsides are covered with heather and bracken or undrained bog, swept by wind and rain. The physical conditions have always made agriculture difficult, and in the industrial age geographical remoteness from the main English centres and from Europe has been a handicap. For all the lowlanders' gospel of hard work Scotland has generally been some way behind England in material conditions.

During the nineteenth century much industrial development, based at first on coal-mining, took place in the region round Glasgow and Edinburgh—now well over half of the total population is in this small area, and most of it in the western part; although Edinburgh is the capital, Glasgow has for a long time been the chief centre of commerce and industry.

Glasgow is well known for the bad living conditions of some of its districts, notably the area called the Gorbals, on the south side of the River Clyde; but the town has a more distinctive character than any English provincial town. A huge rebuilding programme has already made considerable progress.

Scottish towns look very different from English towns. Architectural traditions have been quite distinct, with certain styles appearing all over Scotland but not at all in England. In the central areas of towns, where in England nineteenth-century building consisted mostly of long rows of two-storey red brick houses, the Scots built grey four-storey apartment-houses. The streets of most country villages have little of the grace of the English eighteenth and early nineteenth centuries. Stone has been the usual building material until very recently, though now brick is often to be seen; in fact Scottish architecture seems to be gradually losing its distinctive character.

The most interesting and beautiful part of Scotland—and of the whole of Britain—is the north and west, or the region commonly called 'the highlands and islands'. Great sea-lochs, or fjords, not unlike those of Norway, alternate with wild and empty hills, and on some of the lochs there are farms which can only be reached by boat. Cone-shaped, boggy mountains of 1,000 to 1,300 metres high, separated by deep valleys, cover the whole inland area as well as parts of some islands. Agriculture is hard and poor. Shooting, fishing and deer-stalking are rich men's sports, pursued especially on estates belonging to old aristocrats or new tycoons of commerce, some of them English, some foreign. The old small towns and villages have hotels and caravan-sites, but the country has not been spoiled by over-development. Most of the main roads are now at least wide enough for two cars to pass, but the caravans make driving wearisome. Aviemore in the Cairngorm region of the Central Highlands is the only big ski-resort. Thousands of holiday-makers visit the Highlands in the summer, hoping for good luck with the weather.

The emigration of young people to the towns is leaving some Highland areas almost deserted, and the maintenance of medical services, regular steamers from the mainland to the islands and all other kinds of communications, is possible only with the help of big subventions from the state. In recent years many hydro-electric power stations have been built to make use of some of the vast water resources of the Highlands, and now North Sea oil development is revolutionising the north-east. Elsewhere communities are kept alive partly by holiday-makers and tourists, partly by rich men who have big estates to which they come up from London for shooting and fishing, and partly by the few who, like George Orwell when he lived on the island of Jura, want to escape from the busy modern world. In 1961–81 the Highland population rose a little, for the first time for a hundred years.

The foundation of Scotland's distinctness from England is partly religious. Calvin's influence at first affected doctrine in England and Scotland alike, but when the English adopted the moderately Protestant system of the Anglican Church the Scots would not follow them. Under the religious leadership of John Knox they fully accepted the Reformation and established their own Presbyterian church, which has survived, with some serious breaches in its own ranks, until the present time.

The Church of Scotland performs the function of a national Church. Its services are relatively well attended, and the annual meetings of its General Assembly are great national occasions. Its Moderator, elected annually by the Assembly, has precedence in Scotland above the Prime Minister. He is not a bishop; there are no bishops, no hierarchy. The Queen attends Church of Scotland services when in Scotland, but has no formal position in relation to it. Its sole head is Jesus Christ. Scottish Presbyterianism has a puritan tradition, expressed in the past by doctrinal rigidity and by condemnation of Sabbath-breaking, the theatre, dancing and pleasure-seeking, but these severities have largely disappeared. It is easier to get a drink than in England, and the pubs close later. Sundays in Scotland, once notorious for their extreme austerity, are now about the same as in England. There is a large proportion of Roman Catholics, particularly in Glasgow, and hostility between Catholics and Protestants occasionally produces fights, usually associated with football matches.

Because of the Puritan influence education was for a long time more easily accessible to the people and more democratic than in England. Three hundred years ago nearly every Scottish community had a good school, and for a very long time after that, while most students at Oxford and Cambridge were the sons of rich men amusing themselves, the four universities of Scotland were full of poor students who had no means or inclination to do anything but study. Some became school teachers or ministers of the Church of Scotland, but many others took the road to England to seek their fortunes and to use the abilities which education had developed in them. This process is sometimes called the conquest of England by the Scots, and it has not stopped yet.

Many Scotsmen have gone to England to seek their fortunes, but many others have gone farther from home. It has been estimated that there are over 20 million people of Scottish extraction in North America, Australia and other parts of the world. Two hundred years ago the typical Scotsman, hard-working, serious-minded and economical, was noticeably different from the Englishman of the privileged classes, who tended to admire extravagance and a certain frivolity, and this contrast may have much to do with the development of the Scottish reputation for meanness. Modern Scotsmen may still dislike wasting money, but most visitors to modern Scotland come away with an impression that the people are hospitable, generous and friendly.

Scottish law, based on Roman law, remains distinct from English. The Scottish courts are organised quite differently from the English, and the law itself is different—though on some matters legislation affecting Scotland has made the law the same in the two countries. Most cases in Scotland are tried in sheriff courts, which have no exact equivalent in England. In the whole country there are twelve sheriffs and sixty sheriffs-substitute, who are advocates who have accepted these paid judicial posts. A sheriff or sheriff-substitute may deal with a fairly small criminal case under summary procedure, sitting without a jury, but he may also sit with a jury to

try a more serious case on indictment. A Scottish jury consists of
fifteen persons instead of twelve, and is not bound to find a person
'guilty' or 'not guilty'; it may find a charge 'not proven'. The most
important cases are tried before courts presided over by judges of
the Court of Session. The sixteen judges of this court travel around
on circuit. They have the official title of 'Lord', but they are not
members of the House of Lords.

For internal adminstration Scotland already had a devolved
system by 1945. Education, agriculture, housing, health, planning,
roads, transport, public order and local government were already
the responsibility of departments of the Scottish Office, under the
political control of the Secretary of State for Scotland, who must
always be a Scottish M.P. Legislation concerning all these matters
has for a long time been separately passed for Scotland. The
Scottish health service is based, for example, on the National Health
Service (Scotland) Act, and the Local Government (Scotland) Act
of 1973 reformed Scottish local government in a way different from
the English, with 'regions' instead of 'counties'.

Although Scottish bills are passed by Parliament at Westminster,
their details are in practice debated only by M.P.s representing
constituencies in Scotland. (Most, but not all of these, are Scots and
some Scottish people represent constituencies in England.) Apart
from their work on bills, the M.P.s for Scotland have for many
years held at least six debates a year on aspects of Scottish affairs (in
a committee room in the Palace of Westminster).

Seeing that more people voted Yes than No in the referendum
on the election of a Scottish assembly, the Scottish National Party
demanded immediate action from the Labour government. The
Prime Minster offered a new debate, but the Nationalists were not
satisfied. They put down a motion of no confidence in the
government. The Conservatives took this opportunity to put down
their own no confidence motion, so the debate involved wider
issues. The government was defeated by 311 votes to 310.

At the ensuing general election the Scottish National Party lost
nine of its eleven seats, with its proportion of the votes in Scotland
down to 18 per cent (compared with 30 per cent in 1974) and they
fared even worse in 1983.

At every election in the past twenty years Labour have won
between 41 and 46 of the 71 seats in Scotland (72 in 1983); the
working of a four-party system since 1974 has had peculiar effects,
as the following table shows:

General elections in Scotland

	per cent of votes			seats		
	1974	**1979**	**1983**	**1974**	**1979**	**1983**
Labour	36.3	41.5	35.1	41	44	41
Conservative	24.7	31.4	28.4	16	22	21
Liberal	8.3	8.7	24.5	3	3	8
Scot. Nat.	30.4	17.3	11.8	11	2	2

4   Ireland

In a book about Britain it is not necessary to speak of the Republic of Ireland, but something must be said of Irish history in order to make clear what is the position of Northern Ireland within the United Kingdom. The inhabitants of this large and beautiful island are mainly Celtic in origin, and the majority never accepted the Reformation. After the Reformation in England and Scotland, however, many English and Scottish Protestants were settled in Ireland by English monarchs and became the most powerful element in the country, owning much of the land, although they remained relatively few in number, except in the north, where they are now a majority.

The full union of Ireland with Great Britain took place only in 1801, when the new political unit created by the union was called the United Kingdom of Great Britain and Ireland. The union was not favourable to the Catholic majority of the inhabitants, who regarded the dominant Protestant minority as foreign invaders and oppressors. In the nineteenth century the island was scarcely able to support the population, and at times many people died through famine; great numbers of others crossed the Atlantic to America. The development of Ireland in the nineteenth century is best illustrated by a glance at the population figures. Between 1840 and 1900 there was a dramatic increase of population in most parts of Europe, and the population of England rose from 16 million to 32 million. During the same period the population of Ireland fell from 8.5 million to 4.5 million.

In the last quarter of the nineteenth century a majority of Irish people were demanding some measure of self-government, or 'home rule', and the Irish members of the United Kingdom House of Commons in London became active in complaining of Irish grievances. Soon there was violence and civil disturbance, and the

*A child plays among the debris of a barricade in
Belfast. Note the irony of the poster.*

Irish question dominated British politics until the begining of the
Great War of 1914.

In the six northern counties the one million Protestants, who
were about two-thirds of the population, did not want to be
included in a self-governing Ireland dominated by Catholics.
Eventually the country was partitioned. The greater part became
the Irish Free State (Eire) in 1922. It stayed within the British
Commonwealth for a time, but remained neutral in the war of

1939–45 and formally became a republic in 1949. Its government works hard to revive the Irish language but in spite of all its attempts English remains the main language of the people in most parts.

Meanwhile the six northern counties remained part of the United Kingdom, but after 1922 had their own Parliament, Prime Minister and government responsible for internal affairs.

Within the six counties of Northern Ireland the political system has never ceased to be dominated by the Protestant and Catholic communities' mutual hostility. Until 1970, the Protestants, being in a majority, arranged affairs to protect their own advantage. Local councils dominated by Protestants appointed Protestants to most local offices, especially the more important ones. Catholic resentment has grown, while extremist Protestants have won much public acclaim among their own people by keeping alive the old hatreds. There is a great love of processions commemorating past confrontations. In 1969 a vigorous civil rights movement began to attack the devices used by the Protestant majority for maintaining their supremacy, and Protestant extremists reacted. There were serious disorders between the two communities and the police were alleged by the Catholics to be favourable to the Protestants.

In August 1969 British troops were sent to keep order, and at first were mostly seen to be impartial. Then the Irish Republican Army, or mainly its 'Provisional' section, began a campaign of terrorism with bombs and shooting in support of its demand for union with the Republic. Hundreds of people have been killed by chance, mostly by bombs left in cars, shops or pubs. The army used special powers to arrest people and hold them in 'internment' without trial. In 1971–2 it was found that some suspects had been given treatment which was not acceptable by British standards. The Government gave orders that such treatment was not to be repeated. Meanwhile, reforms of the political and local government system tried to remove the causes of Catholic grievances.

As terrorist acts continued, including a few done by Protestant extremists, there were differences among both elements, between those who wished to find a workable political compromise with guarantees of democratic rights, and the extremists: Protestants who wanted to dominate again, and Catholics who wanted the north to be incorporated in the Irish Republic. The British central government took over responsibility for Northern Ireland's internal affairs in 1972, in an attempt to find a workable solution. It held a

Above: A soldier stands on guard in Belfast.
*Below: Protestant extremists hold a ceremonial march
through Belfast.*

plebiscite, in which 57% of the adult population voted to remain within the United Kingdom; almost all the minority failed to vote at all. In 1973 a new assembly was elected by proportional representation (so that many different views would find expression), but the British Government kept charge of public order for the time being, to placate Catholic fears that if a Protestant majority got full powers again, it would use them for its own advantage.

The new regime of 1973 was a genuine attempt to produce a system of government and administration in which there are safeguards against communal discrimination. It was accepted by moderate Catholic and Protestant politicians. However, at the Assembly elections and the U.K. general election of 1974 Protestant extremist candidates (opposed to reforms) won more votes than the moderates who were prepared to work for reconciliation.

Until 1972 the Protestant Ulster Unionists sat with the Conservatives in the U.K. Parliament. Since then they have been separate, hostile to all British parties: a kind of Protestant Nationalist in fact—though they still call themselves loyalist. They have split among themselves, and support for extremism has grown. On the Catholic side, successes have been gained by politicians identified with the use of terrorism to obtain the inclusion of the North within the Republic of Ireland; but that solution could only be imposed against the wishes of two-thirds of the inhabitants of the northern counties. This Protestant majority can well point out that since the South gained its independence and installed a Republic with an explicitly Catholic constitution, its Protestant population has been halved, while in the North the Catholic population grew rapidly in spite of the government's being dominated by the Protestant majority. A Catholic claim is that the Protestants are descended from an early wave of colonial invaders; and the degree of separateness of the two communities, through three hundred years, supports this claim.

There is much to foster the hostility between the two tribes, yet there are plenty of people in both who wish to live together in peace if they have the chance. One small item goes beyond pious hopes: the Irish rugby football team is still formed from all sections of the Republic and the North, and a collective sense of Irishness supports it as though the troubles were not happening.

The purpose of the British, agreed among majorities in all parties, is to remove the causes of the Catholics' genuine grievances, and thus to unite the two communities against the irreconcilable extremists. Under direct British rule there has been real progress towards this end. But the British military, in their work against the terrorists, can easily be seen as oppressors; and the rare occasions when a soldier shoots an innocent Catholic in error produce great damage to their real purpose. So long as the British army stays, with a duty to combat terrorists, such tragic events inevitably happen. Yet if the British army left, there would almost certainly be a new wave of violence; and if internal self-government were restored it seems likely that the Protestant majority could seek to re-establish its dominance. The achievement of the policies since 1972 has been to eliminate undue privilege and to keep violence at a level lower than would have been likely under any other policy.

Question
Some people think that it would be unsatisfactory to set up special devolutionary assemblies for Scotland and Wales without doing the same for regions of England as well. Do you agree?

Above: Mrs Thatcher and other world leaders at an economic summit.
Below: Royal Marines engaged in the Falklands conflict.

14

Britain and the World

1   The Commonwealth

The modern successor of the old British Empire is the
Commonwealth, an association of 48 independent states together
with Great Britain. All 48 were at some time under British rule;
each became independent after a period with an internal
government responsible to an elected legislature. The old Empire
had two main types of territories. First, temperate, sparsely
populated lands to which people from Britain went as emigrant
settlers. Second, countries with hot climates, thickly populated
already, to which the British went as traders before imposing their
political rule. This second group now forms a part of what has
become generally known as the third world countries.

The main settler countries were entirely self-governing before
1914. India and Pakistan followed in 1947, the African territories
mainly between 1957 and 1965, and various islands, particularly in
the Carribbean, later. All these are independent states and members
of the United Nations. India began, like Canada, with the Queen as
head of state represented by a Governor General, but became a
republic in 1950. Now 25 of the independent states of the
Commonwealth are republics, while the rest still keep the Queen as
head of state; in practice the difference is normally of no
importance.

Each Commonwealth country, on becoming independent, began
with a constitutional system modelled on the British, with an
elected legislature, based on regular elections and the assumption of
competition for election, a head of state to appoint a prime minister
and government responsible to the legislature. Before long,
however, many states drifted into one-party rule or dictatorship.

Politically, the Commonwealth now means very little. However,
some quite important links survive. There are frequent meetings of

Commonwealth heads of government, with discussions both amicable and acrimonious. In education the links are still substantial, particularly at the level of universities—above all with higher degrees. In sport, the Commonwealth Games have continued to thrive. Visits by the Queen and by members of her family contribute to the maintenance of some sense of shared concerns.

It is not easy to evaluate the Commonwealth in the 1980s. The British parties, in their manifestos for the 1983 election, mentioned it in passing, as though it were a matter not to be omitted; the Conservatives promised their 'full support' and continuing aid; Labour said 'We will strengthen Britain's political and material commitment'.

Since the American War of Independence only one colonial territory has broken away from colonial rule without British agreement. In 1922 Southern Rhodesia, which has since become Zimbabwe, had 60,000 settlers and several million African inhabitants. Internal self-government was granted to a regime dominated by white settlers: a status involving partial independence for a territory which was not like Canada or Australia. In the 1950s and 1960s, while the black African countries gained their independence with agreement, the British insisted that Zimbabwe must have majority rule for an independence constitution. In 1965 the settler regime broke away, and it was not until 1980 that its leaders accepted majority rule, and the independence that went with it.

The main embarrassments for the 1980s and beyond are with those territories where, for special reasons, British rule survives. Like another old colonial island trading post (Singapore, which became independent in 1963), Hong Kong has excited the world's admiration for the speed of its economic progress. The British set up a trading post there in 1841, when it was barren and inhabited only by a few fishermen. By 1984 it had more than five million Chinese inhabitants and an airport with traffic comparable with Amsterdam's. But Hong Kong is Chinese, held by the British on a lease due to expire in 1997. In the meantime its administration is colonial, while the British Foreign Office negotiates conditions for the future with the Chinese government, trying above all to enable the inhabitants to continue their own development without hindrance.

Gibraltar is geographically a part of Spain, ceded to Britain in

1713 by the Treaty of Utrecht. The 30,000 inhabitants of this small promontory have voted, by a huge majority, against incorporation into Spain; they would prefer to become part of the British United Kingdom. So small a territory could not easily become an independent state. There is no clear solution to this problem, unless perhaps a special regime, satisfactory to Spain, with nominal sovereignty transferred to a newly created European Community body.

In various parts of the world, islands remain as British dependencies, mostly with substantial settler populations. For each there is a special reason, including above all the inhabitants' satisfaction with the present arrangements—including St. Helena and Ascension in the south-east Atlantic.

The group of islands further to the west has lately moved to the centre of world attention, and of British political concerns. A French settlement in 1764 from St. Malo gave the islands a name, the Malouines. Soon the French sold their claim to Spain, as the colonial power on the South American continent 400 kilometres away, and for a time some convicts were deported there. In 1771 a British claim to part of the territory was recognised. From 1833 there has been a permanent British settlement, by people of British origin, happy to be administered from Britain yet suffering from their isolation. The British gave the islands a new name, Falklands.

The nearest continental land is Argentina, and successive Argentine governments have used arguments of geography, and some of history, to claim sovereignty, an issue which British governments have discussed at length without result.

In 1982 the British government reduced its small military forces on the Malvinas-Falklands, and in South Georgia not far away. The next part of the story is well known: the Argentine invasion, with a force of 10,000 men, and its eventual surrender, after six weeks of war, to a much smaller British force sent to expel them. The Argentine military junta, responsible for the disaster, collapsed. The new regime continued to claim sovereignty, while the British incurred costs, first on their task force, then on safeguarding the islands, some hundreds of times greater than the small costs which they had saved by reducing their military forces early in 1982.

These events had a remarkable effect on the internal politics of Britain. Before the Argentine invasion Mrs Thatcher's government was deeply unpopular at home. After the remarkable operations of the task force, opinion polls showed support for the Conservatives at a level never attained by any government since opinion polls began. The enthusiasm soon began to ebb, but its remaining effects, combined with Labour's disarray, helped the Conservatives to win their big majority of seats in Parliament in 1983.

2 Europe

After 1945 British opinion favoured the creation of new European links, and strongly promoted the establishment of the Council of Europe in 1949. But in 1957, when six countries set up the European Community by signing the Treaty of Rome, Britain stayed outside. Concern with Commonwealth relationships, and dislike of common import tariffs and the agricultural policy, were at that time serious obstacles. Later there was France's veto, prompted by de Gaulle's intuitive misgivings—so long as he was President.

By 1970 British unhappiness at continuing exclusion was strong enough to ensure that all three parties' election programmes favoured negotiation for entry to the Community. In 1972, after favourable votes in both Houses of Parliament, Britain joined. By this time the Labour Party was divided, The unions and left wing were deeply hostile. The leaders criticised the terms of entry, and the seats allocated to Labour in the European Parliament were left empty.

After Labour returned to power in 1974 the Wilson government solved its problems by holding a nationwide referendum (the first in British history) on the question of continuing membership. Of the three-fifths of the electorate who voted, two-thirds voted Yes, one third No. The question of membership seemed finally settled; Labour M.P.'s took their places in the Parliament and worked with the Socialist group. Meanwhile Britain's Conservative Euro-M.P.s' sat as a separate group, joined by one Dane.

Since 1975 all British parties have agreed in their dislike of the system by which each state's budget contribution is determined, and of the cost, nature and objectives of the Common Agricultural Policy. After losing power in 1979 the Labour Party followed the wishes of its left wing and committed itself to a promise to withdraw. In the words of Labour's 1983 manifesto: 'the next Labour government, committed to radical policies for reviving the British economy, is bound to find continued membership a most serious obstacle ... British withdrawal is the right policy for

Britain. That is our commitment'.

Meanwhile the Thatcher Conservative government in power has in general seemed to behave as though the British national interest must take absolute priority. The first direct election to the European Parliament was delayed by Britain's insistence on the use of single member constituencies. The decision was taken by a free vote of the House of Commons, so late that there was not time to fix the constituency boundaries in time for the date originally fixed. When the election took place in 1979 it produced a distorted representation, with the Conservatives, alone of all groups in the European Parliament, having more voting weight there than their popular support justified, while the British Liberals, with a bigger percentage of votes than the Liberals of any other country, had no seats at all. Two-thirds of the electorate abstained: more even than at recent elections for local councils, and far more than in any other European country. Abstention was lowest in Northern Ireland, where, exceptionally, proportional representation was used, giving one seat each to a moderate Catholic and one each for two rival Protestant groups.

After this experience, and although the main arguments for this voting system are not relevant to the European Parliament, the British government refused to change the voting system, or to conform with agreed Community policy, for the election of 1984.

In the 1984 election the distortion between Labour and Conservative was not as great, but the Alliance, with a greater percentage of the votes than in 1979, still had no seats. The level of abstention was equally high, with 68 per cent of the electorate not voting.

European election results				
	1979		1984	
	votes %	seats	votes %	seats
Conservative	51	60	41	45
Labour	33	17	37	32
Liberal (1979)/ Alliance (1984)	13	0	20	0

Question

Make a case for proportional representation, using these figures in your argument.

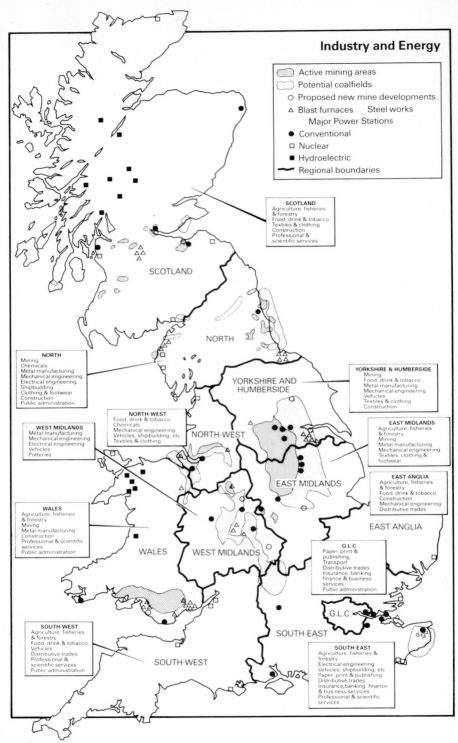

Industry and Energy

Active mining areas
Potential coalfields
○ Proposed new mine developments
△ Blast furnaces   Steel works
Major Power Stations
● Conventional
□ Nuclear
■ Hydroelectric
▬ Regional boundaries

SCOTLAND
Agriculture, fisheries
& forestry
Food, drink & tobacco
Textiles & clothing
Construction
Professional &
scientific services

SCOTLAND

NORTH
Mining
Chemicals
Metal manufacturing
Mechanical engineering
Electrical engineering
Shipbuilding
Clothing & footwear
Construction
Public administration

NORTH

YORKSHIRE & HUMBERSIDE
Mining
Food, drink & tobacco
Metal manufacturing
Mechanical engineering
Vehicles
Textiles & clothing
Construction

YORKSHIRE AND
HUMBERSIDE

NORTH-WEST
Food, drink & tobacco
Chemicals
Mechanical engineering
Vehicles, shipbuilding, etc
Textiles & clothing

NORTH-WEST

WEST MIDLANDS
Metal manufacturing
Mechanical engineering
Electrical engineering
Vehicles
Potteries

EAST MIDLANDS
Agriculture, fisheries
& forestry
Mining
Metal manufacturing
Mechanical engineering
Textiles, clothing &
footwear

EAST MIDLANDS

EAST ANGLIA
Agriculture, fisheries
& forestry
Food, drink & tobacco
Construction
Mechanical engineering
Distributive trades

EAST ANGLIA

WALES
Agriculture, fisheries
& forestry
Mining
Metal manufacturing
Construction
Professional & scientific
services
Public administration

WALES

WEST MIDLANDS

G.L.C.
Paper, print &
publishing
Transport
Distributive trades
Insurance, banking,
finance & business
services
Public administration

G.L.C.

SOUTH-WEST
Agriculture, fisheries
& forestry
Food, drink & tobacco
Vehicles
Distributive trades
Professional &
scientific services
Public administration

SOUTH-WEST

SOUTH-EAST

SOUTH-EAST
Agriculture, fisheries &
forestry
Electrical engineering
Vehicles, shipbuilding, etc.
Paper, print & publishing
Distributive trades
Insurance, banking, finance
& business services
Professional & scientific
services

County Boundaries since 1974

1	BUCKINGHAMSHIRE
2	NORTHAMPTONSHIRE
3	GLOUCESTERSHIRE
4	OXFORDSHIRE

WESTERN ISLES

HIGHLAND
Inverness ●

GRAMPIAN

SCOTLAND
Aberdeen ●

TAYSIDE

Perth ● ● Dundee

CENTRAL FIFE

Stirling ● ● Dunfermline LOTHIAN

NORTH SEA

Glasgow ● ● Edinburgh
Motherwell ●

Ayr ● BORDERS

STRATHCLYDE

DUMFRIES AND GALLOWAY

NORTHUMBERLAND
TYNE AND WEAR
DURHAM
CLEVELAND

Newcastle-upon-Tyne ●
Carlisle ● Sunderland ●

CUMBRIA

ISLE OF MAN

Darlington ●
Middlesborough ●

ENGLAND

NORTH YORKSHIRE
WEST YORKSHIRE
SOUTH YORKSHIRE
HUMBERSIDE

Lancaster ●

IRISH SEA

LANCASHIRE

Bradford ● York ● Kingston-upon-Hull

Blackpool ● Burnley ● Leeds ●

GREATER MANCHESTER Huddersfield ● Grimsby ● LINCOLNSHIRE

MERSEYSIDE Wigan ● Barnsley ● Doncaster ● NOTTINGHAMSHIRE
Bolton ●
Liverpool ● Manchester ● Sheffield ● CAMBRIDGESHIRE

CHESHIRE DERBYSHIRE BEDFORDSHIRE
HERTFORDSHIRE

GWYNEDD CLWYD

Stoke-on-Trent ● Derby ● Nottingham ●

NORFOLK

LEICESTERSHIRE Norwich ●

STAFFORDSHIRE Shrewsbury ●

WEST MIDLANDS SHROPSHIRE Leicester ● Peterborough ●

WARWICKSHIRE Birmingham ● SUFFOLK

HEREFORD AND WALES Coventry ● 2 Ipswich ●
WORCESTER Northampton ● Cambridge ●

Worcester ● ESSEX

Hereford ● 1 Luton ● GREATER
LONDON
DYFED POWYS 3 4 Oxford ● Southend ●

GWENT
Swansea ● AVON Swindon ● KENT
WEST GLAMORGAN Cardiff ● Bristol ● BERKSHIRE Reading ●
MID GLAMORGAN SURREY Dover ●
SOUTH GLAMORGAN WILTSHIRE

SOMERSET HAMPSHIRE EAST SUSSEX

DEVON Southampton ● Brighton ●

Exeter ● DORSET WEST SUSSEX

CORNWALL Plymouth ● Bournemouth ●
ISLE OF
WIGHT

217

Further Reading

The following books are all Penguins/Pelicans and should be fairly easily available in most countries:

BLONDEL, J: *Voters, Parties and Leaders*
BYRNE: *Local Government in Britain*
COOK & SKED: *Postwar Britain: a Political History*
DAVIDSON & TOWNSEND: *Inequalities in Health*
DONNISON & UNGERSON: *Housing Policy*
FLETCHER: *Family and Marriage in Britain*
HOGGART, R: *The Uses of Literacy*
KAUFMAN: *Renewal: Labour's Britain in the 1980s*
MITCHELL, J: *Women's Estate*
RUTTER & GILLER: *Juvenile Delinquency*
STREET, H: *Freedom, the Individual and the Law*
TOWNSEND, P: *Poverty in the UK*
TREVELYAN, G M: *English Social History*
WESTERGAARD, J & RESLER, H: *Class in a Capitalist Society*

The following useful books are from other publishers, but it should be possible to order them:

BEER, S H: *Britain Against Itself* (Faber 1982)
DAHRENDORF, R: *On Britain* (BBC 1982)
DAINTON, F: *British Universities* (Cambridge University Press 1982)
JOWELL, R & AIREY, C: *British Social Attitudes* (Gower 1984)
SAMPSON, A: *The Changing Anatomy of Britain* (Hodder 1982)
STEWART, A (ed): *Contemporary Britain* (Routledge 1983)
TUPPER, T & SALTER, B: *British Public Schools* (Falmer Press 1984)
VAIZEY, J: *National Health* (Martin Robertson 1984)